OUR DESTINY

THIS ADVENTURESOME COUPLE WENT TO SEA AND FOUND A PURPOSE FOR THEIR LIVES

Claude and Naomi Kerr

Claude & Naomi Kerr
2012

authorHOUSE®

AuthorHouse™
1663 Liberty Drive
Bloomington, IN 47403
www.authorhouse.com
Phone: 1-800-839-8640

© *2010 Claude and Naomi Kerr. All rights reserved.*

No part of this book may be reproduced, stored in a retrieval system, or transmitted by any means without the written permission of the author.

First published by AuthorHouse 10/7/2010

ISBN: 978-1-4520-5277-9 (sc)
ISBN: 978-1-4520-5278-6 (e)

Library of Congress Control Number: 2010910284

Printed in the United States of America
Bloomington, Indiana

This book is printed on acid-free paper.

Before You Read This Book

If you are not very religious, we hope it will not stop you from sharing in our experiences as we followed the desires of our hearts.

Be forewarned, Millie changes her name to Naomi halfway through the book. On our Destiny boat trip, we corresponded with a number of friends who, when they received letters from us signed, "Claude and Naomi," thought he had a new wife.

She is the same one and we are still married, after 56 years, and are more in love than ever. We hope this book will help explain how we were able to achieve this.

Talking with Frank Lindley, who was with us on our first boat trip recently, we were discussing the purpose of the trip on the Jacaranda.

"When I was younger I used to wonder 'What was that all about?'" he said, but at the age I am now, I am not as goal oriented."

As we talked, we came to agreement that character was being built in all of us through the experience. Problems that loomed large at the time are not as significant looking back as they were at the time.

The important things in life, especially if it is a life that is committed to serving God, are not the circumstances, but the decisions we make, and the attitudes we develop.

Claude and Naomi (Millie) Kerr

Table of Contents

Chapter 1.	A Vision For Our Life	1
Chapter 2.	Our Vision Broadens	9
Chapter 3.	Helping the World in Brazil	25
Chapter 4.	Helping the World In Montana, the Philippines and China	57
Chapter 5.	God Gives Us the Desire of Our Hearts	65
Chapter 6.	Death and Resurrection of the Vision	87
Chapter 7.	We Weigh Anchor On "Our Destiny"	105
Chapter 8.	Helping the World in America	173

CHAPTER ONE

A Vision For Our Life

Does everyone have a destiny, or a calling, for their life? If I had one, at the age of 29, I sure didn't know what it was. I didn't think about it. Here I was, father of two little boys, Scott and Grant, with a wife, Millie, who did her best to make me a happy home, but I didn't have high hopes for more than being reasonably happy, and maybe have a little fun. What else was there? I hated being bored. Boredom made me become a restless trouble maker.

I was a hard worker, not too smart, but a hard worker. Because of that, even though I started at entry level seven years before, I learned fast and gradually advanced in my work on survey crews. I continued to advance until I was party chief of the Santa Clara County survey crew where I worked in San Jose, California. Not bad for someone not yet 30, who had little formal education. I could have continued, as it was a good job, one I liked a lot, but it seems my life was destined to go in a different direction.

The year was 1959. I had been reading some books, such as *The Ugly American*. It was about how some Americans living in foreign countries have ugly ways of complaining about everything that isn't the way they have it at home. Others adjusted to other cultures, making friends and helping the people.

Another of my favorite books was about a man who built his own sailboat. He wanted to help the world, so he sailed out into the restricted area of Bikini Island in protest of atomic bomb

1

tests. He was arrested, jailed in Guam, and his boat confiscated. I admired him for having such strong convictions.

I wondered what was happening to this world. What was our future? What can be done about all the problems? What could *I* do to help this messed up world?

Sailboat cruisers often write books about their voyages, and I was fascinated by their stories of traveling to many different countries by boat. I didn't stop until I had read every book in the cruising section of the library. Fortunately my wife Millie, had the same feelings. She also wanted to change the world, and was adventuresome as well. That was one of the things that attracted me to her.

Millie speaks for herself.

I was in my last year at San Jose State College when Claude and I began dating. I was a journalism major. Claude had quit college to take a steady job with a local surveyor. I was 21 and he was 24. In the 50s that was the usual time to marry.

We were both impetuous. For example, one sunny day in early spring he came over in his MG sports car with the top down.

"Its a beautiful day. Lets go to the beach and go swimming!" I suggested.

"Great idea," he agreed, and we were off towards the coast. The ocean water was so cold our teeth were chattering. That didn't discourage us. We warmed up with spicy chili beans and hot coffee.

We were married within a year. On our honeymoon we stopped in Santa Barbara, California, my birthplace. Here the Santa Ynez Mountains cascade directly down to the beach where many sailboats berthed at the yacht club's marina.

"My brother Dick and I used to want to visit the channel islands off this coast," Claude said dreamily.

"We used to see them on clear days," I remembered, "and I always wished I could go there too. I have an idea, I offered, "Let's go to the library. I used to go there when I was a little girl. We can do some research on the channel islands."

One of the articles we found gave the name of a local attorney who owned one of the islands. He requested that anyone wanting to visit the island should get his permission. We went to visit him, and got his permission to visit the island. I expected to go there that day.

Looking at it more realistically, Claude said, "How could we go there? We don't have a boat."

We were just as impetuous about raising a family. Our first son, Scott Edward, was born a little over a year later, then Grant Rodrick 19 months after that.

When he read cruising books Claude shared his armchair discoveries. I identified with the couples he told me about who sold their homes in order to buy a boat. I even found time between changing diapers and feeding babies to read a couple of the books myself.

I had the usual questions. "What if the boat tipped over?" and "How do you sail when the wind is against you?" and got satisfactory answers. The lead in the keel under a boat causes it to right itself. Though the occupants get wet they survive. There is a way of sailing against the wind called tacking, sailing back and forth angling towards the direction of the wind.

One day, after we traded the MG in for a VW bug, we were driving to the beach with our boys when Claude presented one of his creative ideas.

"What if I retire early, while we still have strength, sell our house, and buy a cruising sailboat? It would be our home, and we could travel in it, too."

Immediately the idea gripped me. It was a thrilling idea. I, too, wanted to be able to help people in other countries.

As time went on I went back to school and earned a teaching credential. We agreed that it was more desirable for me to be with our children during their formative years than for me to get a job. In fact, I believe Claude needed my full attention as well. This is one reason our marriage has lasted a lifetime!

Claude describes a backyard boat building project

I have always put a lot of thought into setting goals, then planning years ahead. People have called me a pioneer, a visionary. I offered to help Leonard Massey, a middle aged man who was building a 35 foot cutter in his backyard.

For a year I went and helped him every Saturday. In the process I learned something about how boats are built. Seeing how much work it required, I decided I would rather buy a boat than build one myself.

In the summer Mr. Massey let me borrow his 20 foot sloop, *Stopgap*, named for something you sail while waiting to finish your cruising boat. A sloop has two sails, a mainsail and a smaller jib in front. The *Stopgap* was moored in Capitola, on the coast on the other side of the Santa Cruz Mountain Range.

My brother Dick came down from Oregon during his break from the university. It was during the cold war years when Russia was building the Soviet empire, and he was studying Russian and history. He wanted to learn to sail, too.

"Its boring just sailing back and forth. Lets take a day to sail across to Monterey," Claude suggested.

Early the next day we started out. The ocean swells were so big we couldn't see the mast of another small boat sailing nearby. For us new sailors that was a little scary. We didn't take time to go ashore in Monterey but turned back to return to Capitola.

Dick, who was always looking for fun, wrote a note in Russian, saying he was a captive in distress, put it in a bottle, capped it, and threw it overboard.

We arrived in Capitola after dark. The boat taxi had left for the day. The only way to get from our mooring to the beach was to swim. We blew up air mattresses, rolled up our clothes, put them in front of us, and started paddling.

"Hey, wait for me," Dick yelled, "I'm tangled up in the seaweed!"

He got free and kept paddling towards the beach when we saw the glare of a policeman's flashlight on shore. Dick, now playing the part of a spy, said something in Russian.

Of course the officer didn't understand him, but just called out, "Are you the Kerr boys?"

It turned out that Millie had gotten worried when we didn't return by dark and phoned the Coast Guard. They told her to call the local police department.

Our pleasant sailing that summer ended in an unfortunate mishap. We received a phone call from the harbor master. There was an unusual early storm in September before the boats were hauled out for the winter. The waves washed over the wharf and all the boats were driven ashore and wrecked.

I went to Capitola and walked along the beach. I found the boat. It was beyond repair, but fortunately Mr. Massey was not upset.

"These things happen," he said.

Wanting to learn more about sailing, I went out with Dr. G.I. Smith, to crew on a Thistle, a fast racing boat. To buy a boat like his was out of the question. It cost more than we could afford and we couldn't tow it with our little VW. He advised me to get a smaller, racing class boat.

"Get into racing," he said, "then you will really learn to sail and become a good sailor much sooner."

Not long after that I found out there was a newly formed sailing club in San Jose, our hometown. An El Toro fleet of one-man eight foot sailing dingys was being formed. It was perfect for us to learn to sail.

My friend Jim Riley and I built our boats together in his garage. When it was time to paint and varnish I brought it home and put it in the dining room between two chairs. Millie objected, but we had no garage. When I explained I didn't want dust in the varnish she reluctantly gave in.

There was nothing more than one small spot of varnish on the plastic chair seat to remind us of our first boat.

Millie tells of sailing club adventures.

For Claude, Learning to sail *Torito* didn't take long. We joined the San Jose Sailing Club, and soon the competition drove him on. Almost every week I would pack up the kids, who were two and three years old, and a picnic lunch to go to a lake or a beach for the races. We women would talk and the children play while the racers, mostly men, were out on the water. We even sold our house in Cupertino and bought another one to be near a sailing lake in Los Gatos.

Claude's greatest achievement was coming in seventh place of 120 *El Toros* in the Bull Ship Race across the Golden Gate. The starting line was at Sausalito on the north shore of San Francisco Bay. The finish line was at the St. Frances Yacht Club on the south shore.

One of the races was a frightening for me. It was a foggy day and it began at the beach in Santa Cruz and finished down shore a few miles at Capitola Beach. Claude mounted a compass on *Torito*, intending to set a course angling out to sea and back to make better time.

Within the next hour all the boats had come in except for Claude and another man. As time passed I became alarmed. A woman I knew from our Church tried to reassure me.

"My prayers have already gone up. If there is anything else I can do, let me know," she told me.

A sick feeling emerged deep inside. Then a young girl ran up.

"Mrs. Kerr, your husband came in!" she shouted.

Running after her to the water I saw Claude sail onto the beach, but in a moment the mirage disappeared and I stood there looking around.

"Where is Claude," I asked a man nearby. "I just saw him sail in!"

He looked at me kindly, "No", he said, shaking his head sadly, he hasn't come in yet."

An Auxiliary Coast Guard boat took me out to search for him.

"At 4:00 pm our day is over," they said. Then they took me to the pier and went home.

Ann Peniman, a concerned sailing club member, drove down the coast to see if he had come in at another beach, but returned with no results.

Soon everyone in the club had left except for myself and our boys. I remember wondering what I would do if I was actually a widow, and I continued waiting until, to my great relief, I saw Claude walking up the pier towards us. I had never been so happy to see anyone in my entire life! Running toward him, I threw my arms around him.

"I guess my compass was off," he explained, embarrassed by my display of emotion.

He gave an animated description of his adventure.

"I saw a big sailboat in the distance once, and I thought, 'I wonder if they are headed for Hawaii!'"

"After awhile I watched which way the swells were moving and went in that direction. I came in sight of an unfamiliar beach. This late in the day there are big breakers. It was scary! I knew it might damage the boat, but I headed in towards the beach. I didn't dare look behind me, but the boat wasn't damaged at all!

"A couple sitting on the beach said, 'That looks like a great sport! Do you always do that?'

"'No, I sure don't!' I told them. They were really nice. I asked them for a ride, and they dropped me off here."

Claude was energized in that race and in all the others, but when I tried to take the boat out myself I became confused. It was hard to determine wind direction. When I finally got back I collapsed on the dock from stress, telling myself, "I'm too old to learn something new!" Actually, I was in my 20s, and that is not too old.

The sailing club went to a beautiful mountain lake for a camping weekend. It was a nice day, and I took Torito out. The lake was choppy, and every time the wind caught the sail the boat would heel (tip to one side) and take in water. After bailing the water out several times I tried sitting on the rail to counterbalance the force of the wind on the sail. It worked, and I began to have more success.

We had another campout with the group at Tamales Bay, north of San Francisco Bay.

"I think I'll go out for a sail," I told Claude.

Shortly after I began to sail, the wind picked up. It was late afternoon when it is common to have stronger winds and I was worried! I was sailing well, but was afraid to come about in order to turn around, so I headed for the other side, hoping there would be people to help me in case I capsized.

I came about without mishap, and on the return trip I became exhilarated with success. I sat on the rail the whole time, singing and enjoying myself. It felt good to overcome fear!

Claude was proud of my performance in the Pizzano Race at Monterey. The men were to sail the main course, return, and bring the boat in to the beach. Then it was the wife's job to sail out a short distance around another marker, and come back to the finish line.

Several others passed Claude, but I was the first woman to make it around the marker, since the others were new to sailing. We won a dinner for our family at an expensive restaurant overlooking the sea, and a hair styling for me as well.

CHAPTER TWO

Our Vision Broadens

Santa Clara County in the 50s and 60s was in a building boom, and the engineering department where I worked was keeping very busy. My job was challenging, because we were building expressways and overpasses, a challenge to all of us. Even so, I still longed to go to sea and do something to help this "messed up world."

One day I was musing aloud. "I'd be a missionary, but I don't know anything about that kind of thing."

"You could learn," Millie suggested.

In 1964 I had a terrific crew. The four of us surveyors worked together so well we were able to put out more work than any of the other crews. We also became good friends. We were all shocked when George Morris, one of my favorite men, came to work one day and announced he was going to quit. He had been diagnosed with a rare bone cancer and the doctors only gave him six months to live.

Maury and Ely Long, a couple from the Methodist church we were attending, invited us to a meeting at their home where they were "learning to pray."

We met every week. One time the meeting was held at our house, but only Ely showed up.

"We are looking into something that helps people pray," she told us. "It's called speaking in tongues."

That sounded interesting to me, but when they decided to start studying the Bible I didn't want to continue. I thought we got enough of that at church. Ely phoned to remind us of the next meeting. When I told her I would not be there, she responded, "Claude, we love you, and we really want you to be with us."

I decided to go after all. It was a night that changed our lives. Ely and Maury prayed as though they knew who they were talking to. Then Ely sang, not in English, but in a beautiful language.

"This is what they call speaking in tongues," she said, "it happened in the first century church when the Holy Spirit came on them, and it's happening to a lot of people again!"

"We have been praying for a six year old boy who has leukemia," Maury said, and his blood count has improved ever since. God still heals the sick today!"

Hearing that God could heal people with terminal disease motivated me to want to receive the Holy Spirit. I asked Maury where I could get prayer to receive. He told me where there was a home prayer meeting, and we went there. A man put a chair in the middle of the room.

"Here is the prayer chair. Who would like prayer?" he asked.

I was the first one to respond. I sat in the prayer chair.

"What do you want prayer for?" he asked.

But I forgot the name, "Holy Spirit," so I said, "I want the Spirit of Jesus."

"That's a good request!" he exclaimed.

Everyone there surrounded me and placed their hands on my head and shoulders, asking God to give me what I wanted. It felt like something exploded inside. I cannot say what came out of my mouth next, but it happened immediately: I began to speak in a deep voice and a foreign language. I sounded like an African attorney fighting a case in court.

When I stood up, all the men who had prayed for me began to hug me and slap my back. I felt a wonderful love that I never experienced before, flooding my body.

At work I was smiling so much my cheeks hurt! I even had a pain in my neck from holding my head up, and although we usually cussed a lot, I stopped doing it.

"I took longer," Millie

When Claude spoke in tongues I was struck with almost a fearful awe. I had been wanting the same thing, so I sat in the prayer chair next, but to my disappointment, nothing happened. Claude had never gone to church before we were married, but I attended my parents' church, sporadically at times, when I was a child until I left home.

"Be still and know that I am God," was printed at the top of our church bulletins that were passed out every Sunday when I was a child. That training seemed to hinder me from receiving like Claude had.

As I sat in the prayer chair, I wanted to speak in tongues, but, to my disappointment, nothing happened. When we got home I was too excited to sleep, but lay in bed, wide awake. In the afternoon I laid down to rest.

Claude came in. "Please, pray for me to receive the Holy Spirit," I asked him.

"All you have to do is open your mouth like this," he said, and as soon as he opened his mouth out came the African language!

"No, I mean, just open your mouth." He showed me how, and it happened again.

We laughed and that broke the ice. "God, give her the Holy Spirit," he prayed.

I opened my mouth, "Ahhhhhhhhhhh......," I sang. It sounded like *do ra me fa so la te do*, but without words.

"That's not it," Claude asserted, his smile radiating. It's supposed to be a language.

We kept on going to the house meeting. They loaned me a book to help me in my search for God. I read a chapter about making a commitment to God. I got on my knees.

"God, take my life," I said. "I dedicate myself to you." I heard a cracking sound behind me coming from a picture of Jesus on my bureau. I felt like a bolt of lightning had hit the picture, moved across the floor, and went up my spine.

Another evening I went to my room again and knelt by the bed.

"You need to go to the cross and confess your sins," Maury had told us. Growing up in my old church no one told me I had to do that.

"I don't know how to confess my sins," I said, "But if you help me, I will."

Immediately I received the revelation that the sin I needed to confess was that I never had accepted as fact that Jesus had died in my place for my sins! As I wept, I felt God accepting me, and that he was very pleased.

I didn't stop seeking to have the same experience as Claude. One night I went into the living room in the dark to pray. A timber above the ceiling creaked. I thought of the Old King James name for the Holy Spirit, "Holy Ghost."

"But I'm afraid of ghosts!" I said.

Inside my heart Jesus reassured me, "It is I!" I remembered the story I had heard in Sunday School. During a storm Jesus was walking on the water in the dark towards the boat full of terrified disciples.

"Its a ghost!" they shouted.

"Don't be afraid, It is I," said Jesus.

Another day I walked around the corner to the lake with my old Bible that had been given me in Sunday School many years before, and read about the resurrection of Jesus. Maury had spoken in tongues to demonstrate his language, and it was loud and strange. But I wanted it so bad I said to God, "I don't care if I crow like a rooster, I want everything you have for me!"

Two weeks after Claude received the Holy Spirit we were invited to a breakfast meeting in a hotel. After breakfast someone led the group in singing a chorus, "Oh how I love Jesus."

I had never lifted my arms in praise, but I asked God to help me. Immediately my hands began to rise against gravity! The song I sang was not the same as everyone else was singing. I felt a powerful thrill going through my entire body.

"I heard you singing in the Spirit!," said our friend David Wray. I stared at him, because I had never heard of that before.

I went into a side room and sat down where people were praying for the baptism. A man standing in the back had his eyes closed, his hands lifted, gently laughing and speaking quietly in tongues.

Two ladies came up behind me and grabbing me, began to pray loudly over and over again, "Shundah mahundah!"

Aggravated, I stood up and went to the side of the room to climb up and sit on a table where they could not get to me. Lifting up my hands again I let the song flow out. It was purely spontaneous, like a dam broke inside of me. Joy was flowing through me. I knew I had just been filled with the Holy Spirit!

All the rest of the day I felt delightfully inebriated. A preacher gave examples of impossible prayers being answered. I was stimulated to ask that my brother Roger and his wife Del would write me letters. That was impossible. They had never written me before and had never visited me, so I also prayed they would visit me and I could share with them what had happened to me.

The very next week I received letters from both of them and they came from out of town to visit me. I shared everything that had happened to us.

My sister, Dorothy, and her family came from Southern California for a visit with their two children. Kathy was a bright ten-year-old. They were blessed with a special child, Maryann, eight, who was mentally challenged. I asked permission of Bill, my brother-in-law, to take her for healing prayer.

One of the men who had prayed for Claude when he received the Spirit was a school principal who prayed for children. On the way to his home I asked Marianne, "Would you like to be smart?"

"Yes!" she answered.

"Jesus can make you smart!"

The principal placed his hand on her head and prayed, "Jesus, give her a sound mind."

Today Marianne is in her fifties. She loves Jesus and will not copy the immoral lifestyle of others in her program for the mentally challenged. Her mental capacity has improved, and she is much "smarter" than so called "normal" people who refuse to believe in God.

Scott was eight and Grant was seven when they saw the obvious changes in their parents. We tried to communicate our newfound beliefs. Scott picked up on the reality of God. One time he was sick.

"Do you want Jesus to heal you?" Millie asked him.

He said he did, and she placed her hand on his head and prayed. He immediately got up and ran outside to play. It was not long after that when he was ready to pray and ask Jesus into his heart.

Although we had never prayed in front of the children before, we began asking the blessing before we began eating our meals together. The boys soon learned how to pray, and we asked Grant to ask the blessing.

"Jesus, come into my heart!" he prayed.

It was amazingly easy and natural for them to make a decision that we had to wait for until we were in our 30s!

Claude tells how George Morris is healed.

Hearing that God still will heal people today was the main thing that drew us close to God, giving us the desire to receive the Holy Spirit. As soon as we could, we wanted to go to the Salton Sea in southern California to where George and his wife had moved after he retired from my crew. Even though the doctors had not given him hope for a long life, we believed that if we could pray for him in person, God would heal him.

We had sold our VW bug and bought a classic 1940 "woodie," a wood paneled station wagon. We packed up our family and took off for a three day weekend with George. After a 400 mile trip we found their Mobile home isolated in the sandy desert, but they were not there. The letter we wrote telling them we were coming was still in the mailbox. Scott and Grant were running around exploring the desert. I was depressed and discouraged.

"We came all this way for nothing!" I complained.

"Don't be discouraged," chirped Millie, "We can pray! You know God can do anything!"

I doubted that would change anything, but bowed my head and prayed, "God, please bring George and Otama home."

"Claude, look!" Millie cried.

Opening my eyes, I saw a pickup truck with an over-the-cab camper turning into the driveway, just as though it had appeared out of nowhere. It was so good to see George again.

We didn't know much about praying, but we had lots of zeal, and loved to talk about what had happened to us. The main thing we wanted to tell them was that God could and would heal George.

He accepted what we said, but Otama said she had experienced God her own way through her personal Indian guru. While George, Millie and I and the boys walked together along the lake's shore in the morning we shared our own experiences, then prayed for his healing.

We did not hear anything from George for many years. One Christmas a card came from him in the mail. At that point he had lived 20 years longer than the doctor's prediction. He wrote a letter filling us in on his life.

Reactions we received from many other members of the Methodist Church took us by surprise. The reality of God was our main topic of conversation. Millie even went to the minister's office every week and told him everything God was doing among the few of us who had received the Holy Spirit.

While some reacted negatively, others listened and came to our prayer meetings until we numbered eight. After eight months of this Millie and I as well as Ellie and Maury Long, were called before a committee.

"We are the committee that helps with communication between the reverend and the people," explained the chairman.

Indignant, Maury spoke up. "I want to know what we did wrong!" he demanded.

It was brought out that Claude had talked with some of the Methodist young people in the parking lot, inviting them to attend a meeting at another church. It was a meeting where they could have found out about the baptism with the Holy Spirit that we had experienced. Other similar complaints were aired. Finally they told us to stop talking with people about our experience.

The next Sunday the reverend preached about speaking in tongues, warning that if they pursued it they would risk becoming emotionally disturbed.

Millie was willing to stay, believing we could win them over. I said, "No, we need to find a church where they understand our experience so we can learn and grow."

We visited a number of churches. In March 1965, we found a struggling little group in a church called Gospel Temple. Ernest Gentile, the pastor, had left a Pentecostal denomination to join in a revival movement that started in Canada and had swept across the country.

There were not a lot of people, but the presence of God was there, and that is what counts. During the singing there were times when voices would rise and fall in harmonious melody as they all sang in the Spirit.

"I see two companies of people," said Ernest. With his eyes closed he continued describing the vision. "One is an army of ragged, deformed, sick and sad people marching laboriously with chains on their ankles.

"The other group is small, but filled with joy. Some people in the large group see them and break away, chains dropping off as they join them."

Scott, who was nine, and Grant, eight, loved to be there. Upon entering the building one Sunday morning Grant felt God's love.

"Could we live here?" he asked.

From then on we were there every time the doors opened, Sunday morning, Sunday evening, Wednesday evening, and again on Friday, we learned things about God and the Bible. God often spoke in prophecy through different people.

At work I was grateful to God for some substantial promotions. Rather than working overtime every Saturday, I opted to let my crew work without me so I could be home with the family.

In the days before safety precautions for surveyors, I whistled worship songs while working in the middle of traffic. One day Jay, a man on my crew, was whistling one of the same songs I knew. I asked where he learned it. He didn't know.

When we attended the Methodist church we weren't true believers. We had put a few dollars a week into the offering, but now we gave ten percent of my take home salary as soon as I was paid. We did whatever needed to be done at the church, whether it was teaching Sunday School or remodeling the building.

Our church had a half hour prayer meeting before every service. I prayed during a meeting at church that I could find my step father, Chuck Heddy. He was always moving and I had not seen him for years.

That evening Barbara Croxen, a young woman, went street witnessing with us. I looked across the street, and there she was talking with my step father!

"He told me he had his own tracts and he was on his way to the Baptist Church," she said.

From then on Chuck and my half brother Steve again became a part of our lives.

Because of this exciting new life we had discovered, we didn't have time for sailing. I still loved boats and sailing, but put it on the back burner. We were too busy with what was more important to us, with no regrets, and no looking back. The boats were gathering dust in the backyard, so we sold them.

Towards the end of the 60s there was a prophecy and vision given in our church. Ernest saw an ominous black cloud entering the San Francisco Bay through the Golden Gate. It was an evil presence filled with demonic spirits. These were influencing the minds of young people. Only the young people who were filled with God were not influenced. The cloud kept spreading into the Bay Area, all over the United States, and then to other nations, until it filled the world.

At this time we began to see the first hippies appearing on the streets of San Jose. The young men grew beards. The young women wore long skirts, had long hair, and did not use makeup. They walked the streets or hitchhiked. They came from all over the country to San Francisco for the "Summer of Love." We knew the true love and peace they were looking for is in Jesus, and they would never find it through LSD and marijuana!

Three of us men went to Haight and Asbury Streets in San Francisco every Saturday night to talk to them.

"What can I say to them?" I asked the others on the way up to the city.

They didn't have any answers, so I asked God, "What can I tell them?"

"Tell them I put desires in their hearts, and I will fulfill them. I didn't make them to be monsters that could never be satisfied in life," He told me.

I told them that, and a group would gather around me to listen.

All this was good experience in learning how to approach strangers with the good things God has for us to share. We could always find some who were willing to listen, no matter where we went.

I always seem to be drawn to the younger generation. We reach out to today's new generation the same way.

Millie tells how the peace tract is born.

It was exciting to hear Claude's accounts of witnessing in San Francisco. My heart was burning with the desire to reach out to the young generation myself, but I couldn't see giving them the religious tracts we had been using. I knew what God had for them was what they were looking for, but the usual way of presenting it would not be accepted. I felt that God had a special message for this young population.

"Give them the fruit of the Spirit," was what I felt God was saying to me. "Bait the hook with the fruit!"

God's Spirit produces fruit in lives, and that fruit is love, joy, peace, patience, kindness, self control---all the things that God has. When we invite him to come into our hearts, all of his nature comes in.

Claude and I sat down and composed a message about peace that was short and to the point. Peace comes from God. If everyone had God's peace in their hearts there would be peace in the world.

Louise Pruyn, an art student in the church, drew a hippie design around the peace symbol and the word, *peace*. Our Pastor, Ernest, liked it, and offered to print it for us. We chose blue paper with dark blue ink. As soon as they came back from the printer I took a handful and went down to the San Jose State University campus, just a few blocks from the church. I didn't know it, but a meeting about world peace was about to end.

God had planned that as they left the meeting and flowed out to the street, hungry for the answer to war, I had it in my hand. Everyone reached for it, and I couldn't hand them out fast enough!

From that day I visited the campus frequently. If we could get enough of them into the hands of the students, I believed we could change the thinking of the college community. Next we wrote a *Love* tract. Open flowers with stamens and the word love like a twisted ribbon were printed with purple ink on pink paper. "God is love," we wrote. "True love comes from God."

One weekend we met a couple of students on a hiking trail. I gave them *Love* and *Peace* tracts. Just to see what they would do, I put another one in the campfire they had built.

"Don't do that!" protested the girl. "I like them!"

"What do you like about them?" I asked.

Without hesitating she replied, "I like them because they are written especially for us."

Far Out was the third tract. It conveyed the idea of something unique, a bit like *cool,* and *awesome.* This tract described some of the unusual manifestations of the Holy Spirit.

We approached a young man sitting in a car one day. Claude said, "Here, I have something to give you."

"Far out!" was his response. He looked at the cover. Large bubbles tapered down to small ones gave the illusion of distance. He squinted to read the small print, *Far Out.*

Laughing, he exclaimed, "Far Out!"

During that year we gave tracts and talked to kids from teens to twenties all over town. I would give them out between classes during the day on the campus, and Claude would go in the evenings and on weekends wherever young people gathered.

Motivating the generation of the 60s was a search for reality, real love, real peace, real adventure! We gave them the answers from our own fresh, personal experiences with Jesus.

Claude Gets Over the Shakes

When I was baptized in our new church, Ernest spoke a prophetic word over me before he lowered me into the water.

"I could prophesy this, but I will just say it. I feel this man is called to be a missionary," he said.

Then he prophesied, "The Lord says, 'You are doing what you barely know, I will teach you more, and the time will come when you will no longer tremble.'"

I had always been afraid to speak in front of a group. I was asked to read a Psalm every Sunday morning. Sitting in my chair I would tremble while I waited my turn. While I read the trembling would stop, but it came back when I sat down.

One night I walked up to a college student outside a house where a party was going on.

"Jesus gives you joy," I told him, but my nervousness showed.

"Hunh! You look it," he replied.

Once out of his sight I cried out, "Oh God, please help me!"

From then on I made it a point to smile. One time I experimented passing out tracts without smiling. A lot of them ended up on the ground. Then I smiled while I passed them out. No one threw them away.

Millie's calling to the harvest

"After World War II General Douglas MacArthur called for missionaries to go to Japan," said the evangelist "but very few responded. As a result, Japan is prospering, but the Japanese don't put their faith in Jesus, but in materialism ."

"Pray the way Jesus instructed in Luke 10:2," he said. "The harvest is plentiful, but the workers are few. Ask the Lord of the harvest, therefore, to send out workers into his harvest field."

When I woke up the next morning I prayed as he suggested. To my astonishment, God's voice somewhere inside me replied, "You go!"

I was elated and honored that God would choose to send me. I had never dreamed of such a thing, but I felt great about it! It was as thrilling as the first time something I wrote was published, and I saw my byline in print. Now this assignment, from the great Editor in Chief, outshined that feeling! Such an awesome calling rivaled being the bride at my wedding, even having our babies!

It immediately showed my place in our plan to "help this messed up world!" and I understood Claude had the same calling.

Not long afterwards the same quiet voice spoke to me, "You lack one thing...." from Matthew 19:20, 21.

A rich young man came to Jesus and asked what he should do to qualify for eternal life. Jesus told him to obey the commandments. The Jewish man, who was rich, claimed that he already did, so Jesus challenged him:

If you want to be perfect, go, sell your possessions and give to the poor, and you will have treasure in heaven. Then come, follow me."

I was not elated about that one! I was born during the great depression of the 1930s. We lived in a two bedroom house. My older sister, Dorothy, and I had to sleep together in a double bed, with our brother, Roger, on the other side of a makeshift divider. My heart sank to think of giving up the nice four bedroom house near the lake we recently purchased.

Although I had some hesitancy over that issue, the calling of God became the major motive for everything we did. We were striving to do whatever was necessary to qualify to be leaders and foreign missionaries. We did our best to obey the Bible as the Holy Spirit led us.

The priorities we adopted were to put God in first place, family next, then church and ministry.

At a family camp, "Aunt Emma" gathered the children for a daily Bible lesson while the adults worshiped together. Jim Hay, one of our boys' friends, came up to us very excited.

Breathlessly he exclaimed, "Scott received the Holy Spirit, and when he did, he prophesied!"

Grant also received the Holy Spirit in Aunt Emma's class Both of them received the gift of speaking in tongues.

How God Prepared Us, Claude

In the revival movement we didn't think much of theological seminaries. "Cemeteries," we called them. Since they did not believe in the spiritual gifts we had received, we considered them spiritually dead.

There were good Bible Schools, and I was thinking about relocating to wherever the best one could be found. God knew what was on my mind. A visiting preacher came to our church one evening. He did not know anything about me, but God did.

"I see this brother sitting at his desk looking through college catalogues," he said. God wants to tell you, 'This is the school I would have you in!' The local church is your Bible School."

I believe I learned more in our local church than I would have learned at Bible School. It wasn't head knowledge alone, but I experienced God moving through me in prophecy, praying for the sick, and in street evangelism.

One thing that really impressed me was that everyone in the true church has a function, or ministry given by God. Jesus gives five basic ministry gifts to build up the people who make up the Body of Christ and equip everyone to do his or her work.

According to the Apostle Paul's letter to one of the churches he founded, (Ephesians 4:11) these leadership ministries are apostles, prophets, evangelists, pastors and teachers. They can be men or women.

I asked for a key to the church, and began to get up earlier in the morning so I could go in and pray before work.

"Unless you raise up the five leadership ministries people can't be equipped!," I prayed. "God, if it's your will, give me the ministry of prophet."

During the next few days I began to think about the responsibilities involved. Then I told God, "Please forget that I asked to be a prophet."

It was too late. Pastor Ernest was called frequently to be part of prophetic teams in other churches. The teams were made up of four or five men or women, pastors of churches in the revival movement who were proven prophets.

He took me with him to be part of a team at a church in Portland, Oregon. A couple was kneeling waiting to hear what God had for them.

"I see this couple working hard," Pastor Gentile began, "they are building an iron chain. They are pouring their lives into this work...." He stopped, saying, "that's all I am getting."

I saw the rest of his vision. "The chain is on the deck of a ship. They drop it into the water and watch as it goes clunk, clunk, clunk over the rail, but then it disappears into the ocean, because it was not attached to the boat."

They were counseled that the ship represented the church, and although they wanted to be missionaries, unless they were connected to the church, all their work would be lost.

Another aspect of what God taught me was how to give tithes and offerings. One time I was taking a walk, and praying about giving offerings regularly for missions. I looked down, and there on the sidewalk was a dollar bill!

It was as though God said, "Here's a dollar to get started!"

So I began giving offerings for missions. What I really wanted to do was to keep giving 10 percent of my income for the local church and give another 10 percent to missions, but I couldn't see how we could afford to do that.

The thought came to me that if we sold our house and bought a house with lower mortgage payments and property taxes, we could afford to tithe to missions. Jack Aho, who worked on my crew, had a relative who owned a nice little house on the other side of the town of Los Gatos.

I began to talk to Millie about it, but she said she didn't want to move.

Millie Agrees to Buy the House

In our house near the lake each of the boys had his own room, and there was a spare room where my parents stayed when they came to visit. The little house Claude was looking at had only two bedrooms. The boys would have to share a room. I emphatically said, "No!"

Claude didn't give up, but kept bringing up the subject again and again over the period of a year.

"The house isn't even for sale!" I objected.

Confidently he replied, "But if I make him an offer, I believe he will sell it to us."

Finally, I agreed to go visit the owner and look at his house. It was a older storybook style house with a steep pointed roof. In the backyard there was a guest house with two rooms, each having its own entrance. I liked the house, and being able to tithe to missions finally sold me on it. We made an offer and the owner accepted.

Double tithing brought us double blessings, and we began to see that happen in 1969.

*The Kerr family as missionaries in Brazil,
Claude, Scott, Millie and Grant.*

CHAPTER THREE

Helping the World in Brazil

It had been five years since Jesus transformed our lives. That was when God began to give us specific assignments in his harvest fields. It was in 1969 that our destiny overseas began to take shape.

Ernest was called frequently to be part of prophetic presbytery teams in other churches. The teams were made up of four or five men or women. Many of them pastored churches in the revival movement.

As a person or a couple knelt in prayer the team members spoke to him or her (or both) words of prophecy to encourage and direct them. After Jesus was resurrected, the early church was directed in the same way. The prime example of this in the Bible is Acts 13:1-3. While he was serving in that way in a revival church in Oakland God spoke to Ernest in an audible voice.

"Send the Kerrs to Brazil," he said.

"But they aren't ready!" Ernest protested.

"You have a year to get them ready," was the divine response.

The only other time that he had heard God speak in an audible voice was when he told him to leave Spokane Washington to go to San Jose California and start a church. He told the audience what God said, but cautioned them not to mention it to us until he had a chance to talk to us himself.

The next day, Saturday, Claude was working at remodeling the church building when Ernest asked him to come into his office. After telling him what had happened in Oakland he asked, "Would you be willing to take your family and move to Brazil?"

Without hesitation Claude answered, "Yes!" Then he went home to break the exciting news to me.

He Smiled, I Wept!

In those days I (Millie) had been helping a young Korean woman who had begun attending our church. The newspaper had reported a tragedy that had just happened in her family. Her husband had been shot and killed by his own teenage son in the family home.

The boy, her step son, was convicted and sentenced to Juvenile Hall. This left her to raise their three year old daughter alone. She asked me to take her to the factory where her husband had worked to pick up some things he had left in his locker.

Driving her there was no problem, but when the secretary placed his tool kit and work clothing on the desk. My new friend's eyes filled with tears as she sensed the familiar smell of machine oil and saw his toolbox.

I felt her pain, as the secretary looked at me and said, "This is very difficult, you know."

My sorrow from identifying with her was still fresh when Claude came home from working at the church that Saturday Morning.

"I have something to ask you," he blurted out, but when he tried to tell me the good news he broke out in an an irrepressible smile, and was unable to speak.

He tried again, grinned and couldn't finish.

Finally, when he was able to speak, he said, "Ernest asked me if I would be willing to take our family and go to Brazil. I said yes! I knew you would be happy to go!"

It was the deep desire of my heart to be a missionary in a foreign country, but at that moment the possibility of Claude or one of our children dying or being killed suddenly flooded my soul, and I burst into tears.

Whenever I cried in front of Claude, he would leave. "There is nothing I can do," he explained.

During the following year I spent much time in fasting and prayer. During one of my times alone with God I heard his quiet voice, "Believe in the Lord and believe in His prophets," then I found it in the Bible, 2 Chronicles 20:20. This reassured me that God had truly spoken to us to go, and that was all that mattered.

From that time on, I looked forward to leaving with joyful anticipation!

Claude's Preparations for Travel

Our passports were the first thing we needed to take care of, then we went to the closest Brazilian Consulate office, which was in San Francisco.

"We don't give missionary visas," stated the dark haired man across the counter.

"Isn't there any way we can get visas?" we asked in amazement.

He said it would only be possible if we were part of a denomination that already had churches in Brazil. That was not the case with us. There were many churches in our fellowship, but we all had agreed not to turn it into an organization of any kind.

Nevertheless, trusting God, we went ahead with our travel plans.

Comparing the cost of airlines with boats, we discovered a Japanese line that ran passenger freighters from Tokyo, picking up passengers in San Francisco and Los Angeles, then embarking for Brazil and Argentina. It took 20 days for the trip to our destination, Santos, in the state of Sao Paulo. En route we would pass through the Panama Canal.

We bought second class tickets which included a cabin for the four of us and three substantial meals a day in the second class dining room. There was one dining room for Japanese passengers and another for North and South Americans, so that everyone could have their native foods. It was $60 less than airlines, and provided 100 cubit feet of luggage space. Considering food and lodging for the 20 day trip were thrown in as well, it was a good deal.

What were we going to take with us?

Jim Teasley, who had been sent to Brazil with his family by the revival church in Long Beach, California, gave us some advice, "Go through your house and make a list of anything that you feel you can't live without."

We did that, but the only things on the list were a waffle iron and pizza pans, so Millie could make our family's two favorite foods.

What else did we need to do? We needed something to pack things in, so Claude bought several large steamer trunks and four leather carryon suitcases. We could get everything in these, but what things?

First we took several trips to the dump, then had a big yard sale. Scott, now going into 8th grade, and Grant, 7th, managed the sale and proudly turned the proceeds over to dad to use for the trip. We had two cars to sell. One we arranged to turn over to the new owner after we drove to the airport.

When it came to actual packing, since I am the main planner in our family, it was up to me. Of course Millie and I talked about everything. I kept a list of all the items as I put them in each piece of luggage. I was told this would make it easier to go through the customs inspection when we arrived in Brazil.

Praying about the visa problem, we felt we should seek advice from the Teasleys.

"That San Francisco consulate refuses to give visas to missionaries. Go to the one in Los Angeles. You can get visas there," Jim said.

It was not until the eve of our departure to Los Angeles that we mentioned the visa problem to Joy Gentile, our pastor's wife.

"Well if that isn't faith!" she laughed. "You are leaving and you don't have visas!"

We went to Los Angeles to board the boat instead of San Francisco, and the consul there was happy to grant us student visas, saying he could have given us permanent visas if we had applied sooner.

Millie Relates the Family's Reactions

After telling them that we were going to Brazil as missionaries, I asked Scott and Grant how they felt about it.

"We feel honored!" they exclaimed. Scott was 12 and Grant 11. They admitted they had fears, however, because they had heard about another revival missionary family in Brazil who bought a gun for their boys because they had to go out of town some evenings.

My mother, Grace Killam, could be a bit overbearing, but she had a twinkle in her eye and a lot of love for us children.

One night Grant was visibly upset. "I don't have any friends here, and I'm sure I won't have any in Brazil!" he wailed.

He and his brother had to change schools when we moved into the smaller house, and there hadn't been time to make new friends.

"Well, lets just believe God will give you friends in Brazil!" I said.

I wondered how to break the news to my mother. She was a woman with strong opinions who seldom went to church. Her reactions to our "religion" was not always good.

Once she threatened me, "You had better not go to some country where they don't even have good drinking water!"

During that period of time, a song came to mind that I had not thought of for many years. The words were:

> "Sugar bush I love you so,
> Never let my mother know,
> Sugar bush I love you so!"

Songs have always been one of the ways God communicates with me. To me it meant that I should not tell her, not right away at least. She did not find out for many months. We had already sold most of our furniture and the steamer trunks were in the front room when my mother came up from Long Beach for a visit.

She didn't wait for me to pick her up at the bus station as she usually did, but came to the house in a taxi before I got home. She had never done that before, but I think God orchestrated it so that when I arrived I found her in the living room sitting on a trunk.

"What are you monkeys up to!" she demanded.

"Well, Mom, it's good you are sitting down. I need to tell you something. We are going to Brazil as missionaries."

"Why didn't you tell me?" she snapped, "That is just what I want you to do!"

I trust that God arranged for her to find out the way she did to make it easier for her, because underneath her rough ways was a very tender heart. One time, while we were in Brazil, my older sister, Dorothy, helped her make a international phone call to me. Mama couldn't say a word, but broke down and cried.

Even though I was pleased to be going to Brazil I feared the unknown. I retreated into my familiar occupation of writing. Every Monday I was busy in the church office producing a newsletter, "Gospel Temple Tidings." I couldn't face packing, and left it up to Claude.

I was glad we were leaving from Los Angeles, because my mother and sister Dorothy's family lived near there.

It was July, 1970, when we boarded the Argentina Maru. It was comforting that a missionary couple who had been to Brazil came aboard and visited with us in our cabin. They presented us with a bag full of candy bars.

"What are these for?" I asked.

They laughed saying, "Well, if you don't know, you will!"

Later we discovered candy bars were unknown in Brazil.

There was a Salvation Army couple leaving on the boat, and their church's band was on the dock playing hymns as the boat cast off the lines to leave. The last I saw of my older sister tears flooded down her cheeks as she stood with husband Bill, waving from the dock.

Our boat was tied up next to a huge cruise ship at one of our stops. The Maru was dwarfed in comparison, but it was just the right size as far as we were concerned. Carrying 300 passengers plus freight, it was our home for three weeks. The boys had a great time exploring the ship. Approaching their pre adolescent growth spurt, they devoured the bountiful meals, and visited the noodle bar between meals.

We all shopped duty free at the ship's store. I developed and printed my own photos in the darkroom, and Claude swam in the little pool while the ship lurched through the waves, occasionally splashing water onto the deck.

There were five missionary families and two single women missionaries aboard, all headed for Brazil. The two women were the only missionaries who were traveling in the first class compartment.

One of the men from first class approached us saying, "We are inviting all the missionaries to come up tonight for a debate, and we would like you to join us."

Their contention was that Brazil had been Catholic for over a hundred years, so why do they need Christian missionaries?

Eager to preach to them, I went along with Claude. I said what I had to say, but they were undaunted, and continued to bring up all of their arguments. Claude and the other men in return shared their vision for everyone in the world to experience personal relationships with God.

Conflict is hard for me, and I retreated to our cabin.

When we arrived at our port, however, one of the men who had contended so fiercely in opposition stood next to me.

To my surprise he said, with all sincerity, "I wish you the best of luck on your mission. I know you won't be another Billy Graham, but you will do a lot of good!"

Getting Through Customs, Claude

Lots of interesting and fun activities were provided by the host crew: Japanese tai exercises, flower arrangement, a tea ceremony, a meal on the deck, and relays.

When we crossed the equator they put on a King Neptune Festival. There was a tug-o-war between the passengers and the Japanese crew. Although the Americans were bigger, the

Japanese won the first match, but we caught on how they all pulled together by calling, "Humph, humph, humph!" We used the same technique in the second match and won.

After going through the Panama Canal, we sailed south stopping at Caracas, Venezuela; then, in Brazil, Rio de Janeiro; and finally, Santos, in the State of Sao Paulo. There we were met by Jim Teasley, who graciously made the long trip from Recife, in the north to help us exchange money, buy a VW van and get our luggage through customs.

"You've got a tough customs official," he groaned.

She started with our suitcases. Opening Grant's she tapped on a black zippered case on top of his clothes. "*Que e este?*" (What is this?) she asked suspiciously. Brazilians carried money in such cases.

"*Uma Biblia,*" (A Bible), answered Jim.

She unzipped the case and, sure enough, found it was a Bible!

Next she opened Scott's suitcase. He also had a Bible case on top. She asked the same question and got the same answer. When she checked my suitcase, my Bible case, which was larger, was on top, and we hadn't planned it that way.

When she got to Millie's she tapped her Bible case, smiled, and said knowingly, "*Uma Biblia!*"

As we waited for a taxi outside the customs office she was standing near us. Looking over towards us she said, in Portuguese, "Keep the children off the streets!"

We had just sold our Volkswagen van at home. Almost all the cars in Brazil at that time were VWs. I thought we would get a new model, but Brazil got their dies after they were used in Germany, so the last year's model was the latest one In Brazil.

The money had just been deflated before we arrived, so that a 1,000 cruzero bill was worth one cruzero, about 20 cents in American money, even though it was still marked 1,000. This was a bit baffling at first. Jim took us to a bank, where the teller counted out enough to equal $3,000. He wrapped it up in a piece of newspaper and tied it with string. It was the size of a shoebox.

Off to the VW dealership where we bought our "new" VW bus. Our trunks and suitcases, plus five of us filled the vehicle, which in Brazil was fondly called a *"Combie."* I was glad Jim was driving. He was used to the Brazilian drivers and traffic. I was soon to learn. In the huge metropolis of Sao Paulo it was like a road race. Fortunately, I had driven my sports car in my younger days, so I learned fast.

There were so many foreign missionaries coming to Brazil in those years that a language school had been established in the city of Campinas for the purpose of teaching the language and culture. There were not many Brazilians who could speak English at that time. Now it is quite different. When we returned on a prayer team with healing evangelist Randy Clark in 2001, there were plenty of English speaking young people to interpret.

Later I discovered that the teachers hated to see people of our age arrive. I was 40 and Millie was 37. The older you are, the harder it is to learn a new language. I advise doing it while you are young. Portuguese is one of the more difficult Romance languages.

After the year of training plus several months of working with a private tutor I was praying, asking God how to reach the city of Campinas with our message of life and hope.

"Go to them with my love, and the desire to build them up and help them," God told me, "and they will not be able to resist you."

Dick and Chris Govier were missionaries living in Santos with their son, Jeffrey, 7. We stayed with them the first night after arriving in the country, and very soon they invited us to visit a church in nearby Americana where they were ministering.

Dick played banjo with a Brazilian guitarist, Betinho, who was well known professionally, and preached the same revival message as us. It opened the door for me to teach a basic fundamentals of the Bible class in two churches in neighboring towns.

We knew the Laubach method of teaching illiterate adults. There were many who could not read the Bible or write, so we started a class in one of the churches. One evening a couple of the elders of the church stopped by and were surprised to see what we were doing.

We helped adults to learn to read.

"We couldn't believe it," they told the church when they gathered at the next service. "Here they are, Americans, doing what we should be doing ourselves!"

Adventures at the Feira

The *feira* (fay dah) is the weekly neighborhood outdoor market. Merchants come and set up stalls along a block that has been closed to traffic. Produce, fish, eggs, live chickens, it can all be purchased by housewives or maids.

At our first feira we were challenged by something we saw at the fish stand we thought we would try. We only told the boys its Portuguese name, *jacare* (shoc a ray') . But after they had enjoyed the delicious meat, we got out the dictionary, and they looked it up. It is alligator.

We thought we had come a long ways in entering into the Brazilian way of life, but afterwards, every time we mentioned to a Brazilian that we tried their jacare, they were aghast at the thought, just like you and I would be. Their staple foods were beans and rice. Potatoes, pasta, meat, vegetables, fish, all are side dishes to beans and rice.

The first thing I wanted to do was translate the Love tract into Portuguese. While I was still studying the language the Holy Spirit gave me a uniquely Brazilian way of adapting it to the culture. *Amor*, or love, is fundamental to Brazilian way of thinking. The sentiment covers romance but family ties are strong as well.

We started out by printing 10,000. It was very easy to pass out 1,000 at a time, because few people owned cars. There were thousands on foot in the streets. We got the same positive response there we received in the States, not only from youth, but from all age groups.

Giving a tract to a bus driver, we had to wait while he read it before he left the bus stop. A cashier might read it before she makes the transaction.

One man took a tract from Claude, then returned.

"I need to be saved!", he exclaimed, continuing to talk so fast and emotionally that Claude couldn't get a word in. When he finally quieted down Claude led him in a prayer to accept the Lord, and he went happily on his way.

Millie Continues: Hospital Ministry Begins

Adelma was a 20 year old Brazilian girl, who was working as a maid for another missionary family who were going to the language school. She came to work for us when the American missionary family she worked for was sent to another state. She was a Baptist who loved Jesus.

Every morning I would have her read the Bible to me in Portuguese. Not long after reading the book of Acts she received the Holy Spirit and spoke in tongues, an experience that is unusual for a Baptist to receive. Later we learned that the pastor of her church, who was named after John the Baptist, also spoke in tongues.

After a year and a half our house in America sold, and we were able to buy a little house in the country. It had no street address, so we named it *Chacara Boas Novas*, which means "Good News (little) Ranch." We invited Adelma to move in with us. She had to get permission from her family when she went home to Recife in the far north for the holidays.

One Saturday I felt like staying home to pray while Claude took the boys for a drive. As I knelt by one of the trunks I received a word through the Holy Spirit: *"Santa Casa."*

I did not know what he meant by that, until one morning Adelma came in and said to Claude, "The Lord told me, 'Santa

Casa.' It is the name of a charity hospital where the poor people go."

Then I exclaimed, "God gave me that same word!"

"You and Adelma should go to that hospital," Claude said.

Adelma and I had wonderful experiences praying for the patients at Santa Casa. No one ever tried to stop us, in fact the nurses encouraged us. We would go from bed to bed in the crowded wards sympathizing with the patients and offering to pray for them to be healed.

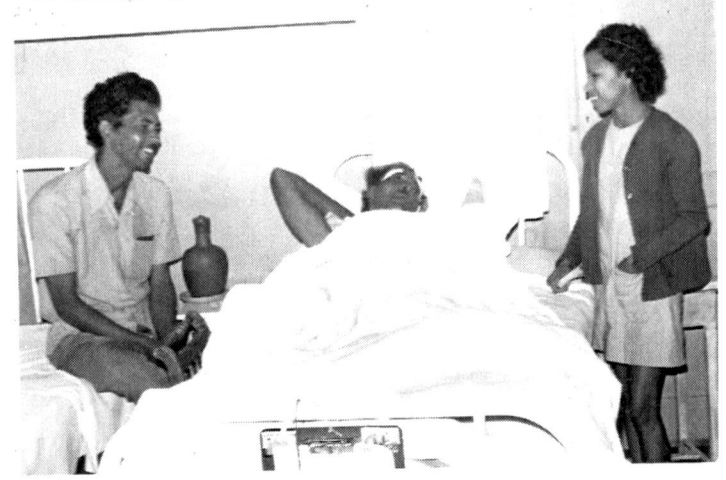

Adelma gets acquainted with a patient.

Before we pray for your healing, would you like to ask Jesus to come into your heart?" we would ask. They never refused.

One time I was speaking to a woman who didn't seem to understand me.

"You have to yell, she's deaf," said the woman in the next bed.

"Would you like me to pray for you to be healed?" I yelled.

"Yes," she said.

"Would you like Jesus to live in your heart," I yelled again.

"Yes," was her answer.

"Repeat after me," and I yelled a prayer, phrase by phrase, leaving time for her to repeat it after me.

Only God knows how many people prayed for healing and for God to live in their hearts that day, because I could be heard for quite a distance!

Claude went into a men's ward another day, where there were about 20 men. He told them God wanted to heal them and wanted to live in their hearts. He asked how many would like to invite him into their hearts.

They all raised their hands in response. Thinking they may not have understood properly, he spoke about what God expected of them, making it a little harder. Then he gave the invitation again. As he led in prayer, there was a drone of voices as every one of them prayed with him.

"There is a prisoner from the jail upstairs. You ought to visit him," a male patient told me one day.

I went upstairs and found a man who had been badly beaten. His eyes were black and swollen and face badly bruised. He said he was injured playing basketball. Obviously he was covering up for the men who had beaten him. Later we learned that it was not common practice at all to send prisoners to the hospital after a beating. Then we knew it was God's doing!

"I have believed in Jesus since I was a boy," he affirmed. "My mother named me after Jesus, Ze da Luz, because I was destined to believe in him. Does your husband preach?"

"Yes, he does," I said.

"Ask him to come to the jail. No one comes any more."

When I told Claude he went to the jail, but came home soon after he left. "They wouldn't let me in because they were doing something with the prisoners," he explained.

This happened several times. I began to fast and pray every Friday while he went to the jail. After a few more disappointments he came home jubilantly showing me a note from the warden in charge:

"Pastor Claudio has permission to enter the jail at any time, day or night."

It was signed, "Felix."

"Felix?" I exclaimed. "That is the name the Holy Spirit told me before we left home."

"Well, he is warden over the jail," Claude explained.

He had gone into Felix's office and God gave him something to say: "You know how life goes. We work hard to get through college. We study something that we feel is very important, because it will help the world. We graduate, get a job doing what we want to do, but we become disillusioned with life, because it doesn't seem to help the world."

"That is exactly how I feel about my job right now!" he exclaimed.

"I would like to pray for you," Claude continued, because God has a good life for you. You just need to experience Jesus!"

Felix consented. After the prayer, he wrote the note. From then on they unlocked the door for Claude every time he came, and he was free to walk through the corridor and talk to any of the prisoners behind bars.

Felix's name had come to me many times and I would pray for him again and again. Now I understood why!

Many of the prisoners came to know the Lord through the 12 lesson correspondence course, which I corrected at home. After completing the course Claude gave them a certificate. One man was almost totally illiterate, so that I could barely read his writing, but with God's help he finished and was proud to receive his certificate.

After talking to inmates through the bars of their cells one on one, during a period of three years, 60 out of 350 prisoners in the jail had written testimonies of their conversions and many had been set free.

I loved correcting their lessons, because I got to read their testimonies.

"Before Pastor Claudio came to the jail I paced back and forth all day, thinking of bad things I wanted to do. Now I am as light as a feather," wrote one prisoner. Many others said they wanted to help Claude start churches when they got out.

"I want to take that correspondence course," one man told him. "Everyone who takes it gets out!"

The first one to be released was Ze da Luz, the one I met in the hospital. He was baptized and became a frequent guest at Chacara Boas Novas.

Ze da Luz

The first thing Ze wanted to do was visit his father. Even though he was a believer in Jesus, he had left Ze's mother and was living with another woman. In Brazil at that time divorce was illegal, but many marriages broke up.

When Ze told his father he had experienced a change of heart he said, "My son was lost and now he is found! He was dead and now he is alive!"

They invited us to come to their home and hold meetings there every week. We arrived after sunset to find a pocket of dark houses. There was no electrical service there. Someone brought out a beer can filled with kerosene and lit a wick to give us a little light as we walked among the homes singing cheerful praise songs.

At one home a woman came out to great us. "My husband had a heart attack," she said. "Would you come in and pray for him?"

We did, and the next week he was at the meeting playing a drum he had made for the occasion. His wife and two grown daughters were with him.

One week we arrived to find Ze's father had invited all his friends from work to celebrate his healing. He had stepped on a nail resulting in a painful infection on his foot. During the night he prayed to God to heal him. In the morning he put on his boots and came out for breakfast.

Surprised, his wife exclaimed, "What are you doing!?"
"I'm going to work!" he answered.
"You can't go to work, your foot is infected!" she said
Then he told her, "No it isn't, God healed me!"

A fellow employee's arm was healed after he prayed, and he asked us to go pray for someone else who was sick in bed at home.

C.L. Preston, visiting from the States, and Claude pray for a sick woman at the healing celebration.

Our Visit Home and Return

Our church, now known as Christian Community Church, brought us home to San Jose for a short rest after our first two years. This church was our sole means of support. People gave so generously that we never had to ask for money outside of the church. Other missionaries at the language school envied us, because they had to itinerate from church to church asking for offerings during their furloughs at home.

We were homesick, and their letters gave us a lift. We received enough to fill shoebox in less than two years. Young people who had come into the church as a result of the Jesus Movement wrote to introduce themselves. One of the young men took us into his confidence and told us about his plan to propose to one of the girls before he even asked her.

Every month, when they received our newsletter, an assistant pastor would read it to the congregation and there would not be a dry eye in the room. After the service there was a line waiting to look at pictures from us posted on the bulletin board.

When our small plane landed at the airport in San Jose California, we looked out the window and saw a crowd of people on the airfield. They held a very long streamer, with the message,

"Welcome Home To Our Missionaries."

"Makes you want to get off here," said a passenger who sensed the love coming emanating from them.

As we entered the terminal building we were looking into the faces of smiling young musicians who were playing rousing music to welcome us. It was gratifying to see so many young people who had been added while we were gone, especially since we had a part in reaching their age group before we left.

Looking back, Claude feels a pang of regret, saying, "We missed out on a revival!"

Tom Hall was one of the young people who we met who was attending Northern California Bible College, a Bible training institute the church started to meet the demand of all the new converts. He and his wife, Catrina, were enthusiastic and wanted to help the world. They had a child, Tommy, and soon were expecting another.

The summer went by fast, and we had to get back to Brazil before our student visas expired.

When we arrived at Viracopos airport in Campinas, Claude came up to me and the boys as we were waiting in line at immigration.

His eyes were frantic as he pointed at the immigration official beside him. "He says we have to get on the next plane returning to the States!" he exclaimed.

I just laughed. It was ludicrous to me that anyone could send us back home when it was the God who made heaven and earth who sent us!

Claude was shocked, but I told the official, "We own a house here, you can't send us back!"

"You were out of the country over the time limit for this visa," he insisted.

"But I was told before we left that we could be gone for three months, and we were only away two and a half months!" Claude responded.

"I am going to keep your visa," he retorted, and disappeared.

While he was gone we got a taxi and went home.

Later Claude came home from a visit to the jail he said, "I asked one of the prisoners why he was in jail, and he told me because his papers weren't in order!" Then Claude laughed and said, "Oh well, if I am arrested because I don't have a visa, I'll have a lot of friends in the jail!" We were illegal immigrants until we were able to get permanent visas about a year later.

Claude posts the church sign.

We Start "Good News Church", Claude

During our visit home we were challenged to start a church in Campinas. This was usually what was expected of missionaries. We found a little storefront space that needed a lot of paint and loving care to make it presentable. Millie and I worked hard repairing and painting.

The space was 17 feet wide and 100 feet long. It was just perfect for dividing into two sections. I made benches and Millie made a curtain to separate the prayer room in the rear end from the front section where services were held. There was a bulletin board facing the street so passers by could look at photos and read about what was going on.

We picked up a slogan while we were home, "Smile, God loves you!" It was appearing on license plates and everywhere else at home, but not in Brazil. We painted, "Smile Jesus Loves You," on our Combie van, the church sign, a tract, and T shirts for the boys and Adelma.

Adelma

OUR DESTINY

Grant

Scott and his monkey, Eliza-betchy

Prophesy was given over us at the last church service before we left San Jose at the end of summer. Several people of the church who had the gift of prophecy spoke words of encouragement over us.

Then they called Scott and Grant to go forward.

"You will go to the harvest field and reap the same sheaves as your parents," was the word for Scott. "You will receive the blessings of the firstborn."

Before he was called forward, Grant had been thinking that when he grew up he would serve the Lord.

"Don't think, 'When I grow up I will serve the Lord,'" one of the prophets said. "You have been like a violin that reverberates with the sound of other instruments being played, but now the master will pick *you* up and play *you!*"

Now they began to work alongside us. Every time the church opened, they were there, praying in the prayer room before each meeting. They both accompanied the singing on their guitars. They each passed out tracks in crowded streets at Carnival season.

Adelma had become like a member of the family. Claude and the boys prepared a room for her, and she was the first member of *Igreja Boas Novas*. Soon she asked for a guitar, and became the worship leader in place of Claude.

Every Sunday afternoon she and the boys played their guitars and sang in a wooded park in town, while Claude and I set up a table for giving the "Love Test." It was a quiz of 10 questions about the love of God to be answered by people who stopped. We then compared their answers with the Bible answers and, if they wanted, led them in a prayer to accept the Lord.

Our Church in San Jose was called "Gospel Temple," but we translated it into "Good News Church." In Portuguese it was *Igreja Boas Novas*.

Before we had our first service at the building we held an outdoor service on Sunday morning in a small square in town that was surrounded by high rise apartments.

Adelma, Scott, Grant, and I sat on a bench, while Claude preached a simple message aimed at bringing the audience to a point of receiving Jesus as their savior. He even prayed a prayer that would complete the commitment to God.

I thought it was strange that Claude would preach just to us, and even said a prayer for the audience to repeat in the deserted plaza.

Two years later a couple attended the church. It was a communion service, and they took the bread and grape juice with us. I was very curious about where they had come from and wondered about their experience with God.

"Have you ever asked Jesus to save you, to come into your hearts?" I asked them after the service.

They answered that they had, and I asked when they had made that decision.

"Why, when your husband preached in the plaza," the lady answered as though she were surprised I didn't know.

My mind went through a quick rewind and I said, "He only preached in the plaza one time, when we first opened the church. No one was there!"

"Oh no! We were listening from our apartment window on the fourth floor," she exclaimed.. "Everyone in the building was listening!"

Only God knows how many others asked Jesus to come live in them that day!

Jesus' Love Makes a Hit, Claude

On the bottom of the tracts there was an invitation to send for our correspondence course. We only got one response outside of the jail, where many inmates took the course, but a man named John wrote us asking to take the course. He completed several lessons, sending them to us when he finished them.

We went to visit him at the return address given. When we met, this is the story he told us. He had just found out the results of his college entrance exam. In Brazil tough entrance exams are given as a requirement for registering in any university. Prospective students study for a year after high school to prepare, and many don't pass. This was true of John. He failed the exam.

"I stood there on the street wondering how I could tell my father. He spent a lot of money for me to go to school. I felt like killing myself!

"Then I felt something hit my leg. It was a piece of paper blown by the wind. I smoothed it out and read, 'Smile, Jesus loves you.'

"After I read it, I prayed the prayer at the end. I felt wonderful, and knew Jesus really *does* love me!

"When I went to my father I told him, 'I failed the exam, but I found Jesus!'

"My father read the tract with me, and he accepted Jesus, too. He said, 'We need to write for this correspondence course and find out more about this!'"

Later we received a phone call from a very irate woman, "I don't want you to ever come to my house again!" she yelled.

Bewildered, I stammered, "What are you talking about? I was never at your house, was I?"

Then she made it known John lived with her, and she was listening from behind a curtain separating another room.

We did not hear from John for several weeks, then we tried visiting him again. I prayed that his girlfriend would not be home, and she was no where to be seen.

"I haven't contacted you because I had some business to take care of. I got married," he explained.

It turned out that the woman he had been living with was a weak Christian believer. When she was discovered to be living with a man she was not married to, the Holy Spirit convicted her of her sin. Her first reaction was anger, but after they were married she supported his newfound faith in Christ whole heartedly.

John Receives God's Power

John showed up at the church one day with his lesson. The lesson taught about the Baptism with the Holy Spirit and speaking supernaturally in unknown languages.

"What I need is the Holy Spirit!" he declared.

"Fine, come right in!" Claude said. We were about to have a prayer meeting, and we will pray for you to receive the Holy Spirit."

Most people who we had prayed for receive the Holy Spirit only said a few words. Others didn't speak in tongues until a later time when they were alone. Not so with John! He received just like Claude did. As soon as we touched him he burst out with a distinct language.

Later he came and asked us to baptize him in water. He had learned what the Bible said about the subject, and after talking with various pastors around town he concluded that I would baptize closer to the Bible pattern than the rest.

Several months passed before we saw him again. He had left town to attend a Bible School.

"They asked me to take a church with their denomination," he said, "but I told them, 'No, my church is Good News Church!'"

We asked him to preach, and he delivered a great message on evangelism. His wife sat in the back row checking each Bible verse he quoted from memory to make sure he got it word perfect. She was proud of him, and so were we!"

Good News Church had a very small congregation. The first to respond was a group of young children who lived in the neighborhood. They were very poor. Two mothers rented two single rooms in an old motel down the street from the church.

When they saw our VW van with the Smile, *Jesus Loves You signs* they would run barefooted down the street yelling, "The little church is coming!"

In no time they had received Jesus, were filled with the Holy Spirit, and knew all the songs in the little song book we had printed. The service would always pick up when they came in. Francisco, 7, was the most fervent of his brothers, sisters and cousins.

Jesus' Cheering Section: Francisco is the boy with his hands raised in praise. The child bending forward next to him had a painfullly swollen foot. His mother told him, "I'm taking you to the doctor tomorrow." "No Mae," he affirmed, "Jesus heals! Jesus will heal my foot tomorrow morning, early!" His mother told us, "Sure enough, in the morning the swelling was gone and he did not need to go to the doctor!" The boy to his far right with the pacifier in his mouth, is Nene. He was hospitalized with a deadly strain of meningiitis. In a few weeks he we back in church. "What happened to you?" Claude asked him. Without hesitation he responded, "Jesus me curou!" (Jesus healed me!)

Francisco's mother worked as a maid and told the lady of the house about her children's excitement regarding Jesus. Her boss wanted to see for herself, so one day the mother dressed them in their best clothes and took them to work with her.

The children called out the numbers of the songs they wanted to sing, and Francisco led them in singing, just like in church. Then this fiery little 7-year-old preached a sermon!

Francisco was sitting on Millie's lap one day while we were chatting with his mother in their one room home when she shocked us with an offer we did not expect.

"Would you like to have him?" she asked. "He is a smart child, and I can't afford to educate him. You seem to like him, and I talked to him about it. He wants to go and live with you."

"But a child needs his own mother. You are the best one to raise him!" we assured her.

Sometimes we think that it was a mistake to have refused.

We really loved him, and he had great potential.

Reinforcements Sent from Home

Things were going well, but slowly. However, we were getting worn out, and requested that the church send another couple to help out with the work. We remembered the Halls, the young family we had met during the summer in San Jose. We had heard that they now had a little daughter, Patience.

The church sent them and they went to language school and learned to speak Portuguese quickly. When Patience began to talk she spoke Portuguese.

"Ah Maria!" she would exclaim, mimicking an expression their maid often spoke.

They enrolled Tommy in the international school, and Tom took over the students' Bible Club.

They brought along a large plastic pool we set up in our backyard where we all gathered for a water baptism. Claude and Tom baptized a teen-age girl and two converted prisoners Ze da Luz, the first convert from the jail, and a 14-year-old street boy, Antonio.

Ze, after being immersed into Jesus' name

It was not long before Tom preached in the church.

Everything seemed to be going fine until they asked Claude to come to their house to talk. It turned out that they were not willing to participate in the jail or hospital ministries nor in passing out tracks. They were disappointed at the small size of the church in Campinas, and wanted to go to the Amazon region that was beginning to be developed. They felt people would be more receptive to change there.

Perhaps they had a good point, but at that time of our lives the work we were doing in Campinas was our entire vision. We had considered moving to Brazilia, which had just been developed as the national capital, but dropped the idea in favor of staying where the boys had a good school.

We had spent years pouring our lives out for the people we had grown to love in Campinas. It broke our hearts that they did not see it our way.

Emotionally, we had hit bottom. Hearing our feelings, C.L. Preston, an elder we greatly loved, made a trip to help us communicate with them. After that, Ernest came down. After spending some time with us it was decided to bring us home and leave the new couple there to run the church.

We asked Ernest to preach to our little group. Claude was proud that he could interpret while his Pastor spoke. He also interpreted prophecy given to one of the young men.

As Claude interpreted, Ernest said, "We feel that missionaries need to come home occasionally for a rest."

Before translating it for the group, Claude's face broke out in a big smile. We were, indeed tired, and the stress of our disagreement was added to our emotional exhaustion.

Scott had already finished his high school requirements and helped get the house ready to sell. A series of miracles helped us.

As we sat around the table talking with Ernest someone knocked on the door.

"Would you be interested in selling your house?" asked a slight-of-build, bespectacled American. He had just arrived in Campinas to take a position at the university. His specialty was insects, he explained, and our neighborhood in the country had an abundance of them!

Two problems were solved at once by him having money in the United States. The Brazilian government would not allow us to take more than $4,000 out of the country. We would have had to leave our entire investment there.

Scott had finished his high school requirements, and was ready to leave, but Grant still had a semester to finish high school, and stayed with the Halls, to fly home by himself at the end the the school year.

In a short time we had sold our furniture and flew back to San Jose where Claude took a position with the church supervising the construction of a complex of church buildings for the church, a private school, the Bible College and a library.

Trying to Understand God's Will, Millie

Following God, we found, is not always a bed of roses. If it is, there are thorns involved. I did not understand why all our efforts in Brazil ended as they did.

"I don't understand!" I told God as I wept alone before him one day.

"Just trust me," was his response.

Now I have learned that he can be trusted. One day, shortly after we returned from Brazil, God spoke to me through the Bible account of how Abraham, known as our father in the faith, was tested by God. He was asked to take his son up a mountain and put him on the altar as a sacrifice to God.

As he raised the knife to make the sacrifice, God intervened.

"Because you have not withheld your son, your only son..."

Then I knew that Jesus understood what I had gone through and the feelings I was experiencing. We had given up something just as precious to us as Abraham's son was to him.

God promised Abraham because he had passed the test, and did not withhold his son, that his offspring would bless all the nations of the world. I began to get the picture that he wanted to use us, too, to bless more than one foreign country.

"We Are Indebted to Love," Claude

The Halls remained with the church in Campinas for a time, but decided to move to the capital, Brazilia. They shared their vision with the group, and Adelma as well as William and Dalva, a young couple who had been with Igreja Boas Novas since it opened, decided to go with them.

No sooner did they begin to make contacts in Brazilia than Tom was apprehended in an extramarital affair with a Brazilian woman and the family had to be brought back home. He declared that he was repentant, and remained in the church.

One day I (Claude) looked out the window of my office and saw Tom outside.

"You are indebted to love him," came the unmistakable voice of the Lord.

I was convicted. Going outside, I approached him and told him, "I am indebted to love you, Tom."

Something happened between Tom and I that day. Healing began to take place. In fact, we went out to breakfast shortly after and had a good relationship.

Later, he fell into worse sin. I didn't see or hear from him until years later. One night I got a phone call. It was Tom. He told me there were five people he needed to call, and I was one of them. He told me that he had come back to the Lord. I was delighted to hear the good news.

Later on, after we moved to Eureka, he came to town to perform a marriage, and we met him there with his new wife.
"You look great, you've lost weight!" we exclaimed, then our hearts sank as he replied, smiling, "Oh, it's the cancer." His smile spoke of the peace he had with God. We met his new wife, and saw Tommy, who was there for a visit.

In 2001 we had a chance to return to Brazil as part of a team that prayed for the sick. We saw many amazing healings. When we returned, I phoned Tom's wife, excited about telling her that we had gone to the Amazon region, where he had had a burden to go.

With much sorrow she informed us that while we had gone to the land of his vision he had gone to be with the Lord.

CHAPTER FOUR

Helping the World In Montana, the Philippines and China

While we were in Brazil, Claude often told me his feelings of abandonment. It was difficult communicating with the home base, being so far away. He also thought we had not been very well prepared for what we were doing.

"A person should be sent out to another state in his own country before being thrust into a foreign culture," he said. "The church could keep in touch so much easier, and give advice when you need it."

When a young couple from Montana visited our church we took them home with us for lunch.

"In Thompson Falls we need a church like yours!" exclaimed the young man. "A lot of us got disillusioned when our pastor left his wife and ran off with the worship leader."

Later two men came from Montana wearing suits and cowboy hats. Rex Denison and Jerry Delmark stood up at the service and asked us to send a team to start a church in Thompson Falls. God had prepared us for this before we left Brazil. The advantage we had now was experience founding the church in Brazil.

We went into Ernest's office and Claude said, "How can we refuse them? "

We volunteered to go and see if a church could be started.

Thompson Falls was an idyllic setting on the Clark Fork River in the Bitterroot Mountains not far from the Idaho panhandle. Growing up in California and Oregon, it was a breathtaking experience for us to see the fall foliage giving way to the beautiful blanket of the first snow on Thanksgiving Day.

We met Donna and Gloria, wives of the two men, and their two families became the charter members of a new church. The population was very small, but scattered throughout the mountains were young people who had come to Montana searching for the simple life during the hippie days.

Claude taught on the basic foundations of the Christian faith, including salvation, baptism in water and baptism with the Holy Spirit, as well as the requirements for leadership in the church. Millie taught Sunday School.

Claude did not feel he had the calling to pastor a church, and neither Rex nor Jerry were ready to take on the leadership. We prayed for God to send someone who would stay and tide them over until they were ready.

God is always faithful to answer prayer. A church in another town in Montana agreed to send a team every week to help them. Just before Christmas we returned to San Jose, satisfied we had laid the groundwork.

Our Sons Grow Up

Our home church started Northern California Bible College on the Church property because of all the fervent young converts coming in from the hippie culture. Scott enrolled as soon as we returned. He wanted to nail down his belief system before anything else.

After two years at Bible college he received his associates degree. At that time I would hear Claude and the boys talking long after I went to bed.

"Choose a career that helps people. Making a lot of money isn't a good reason," he told them.

"Work hard and be honest. What is the desire of your heart? That's the direction you should go."

One day at the dinner table he told Scott he stopped at a construction site, and found out the carpenter's union was taking apprentices. He applied, and began the four year apprentice program.

Since he put God first, Jesus gave Scott the "Desire of his heart," Psalm 37:4. Laurie Dodrill, a young woman from Omaha, Nebraska, came to San Jose earlier to go the Bible College.

Their matchmaker was the Holy Spirit, and they were married the following August. Scott worked hard and bought a house. Later on he took the State exam and got a general contractor's license.

As for Grant, he too followed the Kerr family tradition of hard work modeled by their grandfather Kerr and Dad. His first job was making hamburgers at a fast food restaurant. He showed promise and was promoted to assistant manager. He could have been manager, but was not quite old enough. Bob Radcliff, who attended our church, suggested he apply at Ford Aerospace, where Bob was a manager. They hired Grant, and he began working as an apprentice in precision machining.

Claude describes his vision of China.

We still had a burden for foreign missions. While I was in Brazil I had a dream, a vision that I could never forget. I saw a very large carved wooden door in China. Over it was the word *Macao*. A huge keyhole was in the door, and I had the key that would open it.

I didn't know where Macao was. That day another missionary from the language school gave me an English Readers Digest. I was amazed that in the back was an article about Macao! Macao, I discovered, was a Portuguese colony. It is a city across the bay from Hong Kong which Portugal still governed. Like Hong Kong, which was still under British rule, it was free from Communist domination.

When I saw the vision, in 1970, China was closed to any kind of tourism or trade from other countries. What was known as the "Bamboo Curtain," was the same as the "Iron Curtain," that separated Communist Russia from the outside world.

After returning home, Bob McKim, a Pan Am pilot who belonged to our church, brought me a newspaper he had picked up in a flight to Hong Kong.

I was so excited to see, on the front page, a picture of the gate to Macao! It looked just as I had seen it in my vision. The article said that for the first time since Mao Zedong's cultural revolution, 30 years before, China would open the door to foreign travel through this gate! Government sponsored tour groups would be taken across the border to Communist China through Macao.

"This is the fulfillment of the vision I saw nine years ago!" I exclaimed.

I asked the church board of elders for a four week vacation, two weeks in December for one year and two weeks in January for the next year.

"Where are you going?" they asked.

"I'm going to China," I told them.

I explained that I wanted to go and explore Macao and see if it was God's will for us to move there. We arranged a tour from Macao to south China. Our church had connections in the Philippines, and we took Dan and Susan, two young people from the church to go with us to the Philippines. Afterwards we would continue on into China.

Adventures in the Philippines

In the Philippines many doors were opened to us for ministry. We never could have imagined preaching and testifying openly in school classrooms and government buildings in our own country, as we did there. One day we were ministering in the social security offices, a hospital, and at a millionaires' breakfast, and the next day in the superior court, as well as in college classrooms and several churches, some Catholic.

We got to watch the final day of religious training for a group of Seabees who were being sent to Mindanao. At the time they were fighting radical Muslims, and many who went before had been seriously wounded or lost their lives.

The training was led by Spirit Filled Christian women and a pastor. They led them into genuine salvation experiences with Jesus, and to receive the Holy Spirit. In the final class that we saw, many of the young men took the microphone and testified of feeling peace, love, and joy flooding through them.

The sound of many male voices singing also bore witness:

"God's not dead, He is alive,

God's not dead, He is alive,
God's not dead, He is alive,
I feel Him all over me!
I feel him in my hands,
I feel him in my feet,
I feel Him in the air,
I feel Him everywhere,
I feel Him all over me!"

It was easy to lead the young Filipino people to give their lives to Christ. Several of the churches we visited were almost completely filled with hundreds of zealous, Spirit filled youth. The revival in the islands has continued for many years, and it was an honor to have a small part in it.

The two young people we took with us have continued to go on with their own adventures.

While we were in the Philippines, our schedule was arranged by Teddy Balos. His ministry brought him into contact with many missionaries coming from the United States.

"Where would you suggest that missionaries go who want to help the Filipino people?" Claude asked him one day.

"We have more missionaries than we need here in Manila," he responded, "but where they are really needed is in the outer islands. The island I come from hasn't been touched by the revival message!"

There are 2,000 islands in the Filipino chain. It brought back the thought of sailboats, a fleet of them, going where no other transportation is available.

Exploring China

After three weeks in the Philippines Dan and Susan went home, and we took the short flight to Hong Kong. There we met with our missionary friend, Dennis Balcomb. It was very impressive to watch him, dressed in a quilted Mandarin jacket preaching and teaching in Chinese.

"He speaks two dialects, Cantonese and Mandarin, like a native," a local businessman told us.

From Hong Kong we took a hydrofoil ferry across the bay to Macao. Claude had stayed awake for hours the night before, as he was excited about going to the place of his vision. Dennis had given us a phone number for Doug Sutherland, a missionary in Macao.

"God sent you here for us!" he said. "Becky and I were really getting discouraged, and He sent you here to encourage us." he said.

He arranged to let us stay in an apartment temporarily vacated by a Chinese woman in his church.

We were among the first tour groups to go into China through Macao. We were thrilled as our bus passed through the arch in Claude's vision into Communist China. Claude had seen a door in his vision. There had, indeed, been a door in the days when Portugal first colonized Macao, according to a historical novel Millie had read.

While the tour guide took the group to see the panda bears, we stayed on the sidewalk and greeted people with the Cantonese greeting we had learned at home. A college student conversed with us in English.

"We have to learn English, because all our textbooks are written in English," he explained.

"Do you know anything about God?" I asked him.

He looked thoughtful. "No, I have seen God mentioned in some textbooks, that is all." Then his face brightened in recognition adding, "But there are many Christians in China."

The Sutherlands were in the middle of two years of learning Cantonese. Before leaving home we learned a little Cantonese, but sometimes we were laughed at, or misunderstood.

We had tried ordering a meal in a small restaurant using our limited vocabulary, but the waiter shouted to the cook what we had said, and they both laughed uproariously.

"There are eight tones in the Cantonese language," Becky Sutherland explained, when she heard our story. If you don't use the correct tone you are saying something completely different.

We wondered if God was calling us to China, but after our struggles learning Portuguese and since we weren't getting any younger, we did not relish the idea of learning Chinese.

Calvin worships on the stern of the *Jacaranda*.

CHAPTER FIVE

God Gives Us the Desire of Our Hearts

Before we went to China I, Millie, was driving down the street when God spoke in a "whisp."
"Claude!" He said.
"What about Claude?" I asked.
"Desire of his heart."
God knew that I was familiar with one of Claude's favorite Bible verses:
"Trust in the Lord, and do good....
"Delight yourself also in the Lord,
"And He shall give you the desires of your heart."
Psalm 37:3,4
"What desire are you talking about?" I asked.
There was no answer at that time, but within a few days Claude came home from his job at the church with some news that excited him greatly.
"Guess what! Some fellows came by the church office today who are planning to sail a boat to Belize on a missionary trip!"

We visit the Jacaranda

On the way home from China we stopped in Honolulu for a few days to visit Grace Bible Church. With typical island hospitality, a woman came to us and placed fragrant leis of plumeria blossoms around our necks.

We learned that the church had bought a private plane and planted churches in each of the Hawaiian Islands. They also had a 58' Herreshoff ketch, the Jacaranda, anchored in a bay nearby. A crew of eight had been assembled to go to New Zealand, where it was purchased, and they had sailed it back to Honolulu. The plan was to send it out to Micronesia to reach out to "the islands of the sea," an expression that appears often in the prophet Isaiah's predictions about the last days Church.

We remembered our desire, the vision of 20 years before, to retire young and sail away on a boat to help this messed up world. They were sending the Jacaranda to Micronesia, including the Marshall Islands, where the man I had read about sailed his boat in protest of the atom bomb tests.

It was exciting to visit the Jacaranda, the most beautiful boat in the harbor, glistening with varnished teakwood. We met some of the crew members, including the captain, and his wife. Then we flew back home and I resumed work with the church staff.

Within the first weeks back home our pastor received a phone call from the Pastor of Grace Bible Church in Honolulu.

"Would you consider sending the Kerrs to join the Jacaranda crew for a one year term as spiritual advisers?" he asked.

"Would you be interested in doing this?" Ernest asked me.

"Would I?" I exclaimed, "it's the desire of my heart! But I'll leave the final decision up to the board of elders."

They agreed to send us. It would be a one year commitment, and in the next two weeks I had a lot to do. I had 14 responsibilities in the church to turn over to other people. It all fell into place, with God's help. We arranged to rent our house to a young couple in the church while we were gone.

"I was excited," Millie

I was jumping up and down inside with excitement when Claude asked if I wanted to go on the Jacaranda from Honolulu to the islands of Micronesia. I felt like I did on our honeymoon, when I wanted to go to the Channel Islands off the coast of Santa Barbara, but this time we had a boat to take us! This was even better than I had imagined, because God was behind it. I believe it was he who gave us the desire to start with.

Claude tells about our departure.

God's fingerprints were all over the arrangements. It was He who brought a new couple to the church who were very happy to take over outreach we were having at Crestwood mental hospital. I was praying about who would go to the ranch detention facility for young people when the Holy Spirit flashed a picture of someone into my mind who turned out to be just the right man for the job.

Then we heard about World Airlines, a new company that was opening up with the special promotion of one way tickets to Honolulu for just $60. People in San Francisco were sleeping on the sidewalk outside the office to get tickets before they were sold out. I went to a ticketron in the downstairs basement of Penny's Department Store and bought two tickets, and there was no waiting line.

A week later I returned to the same place to try and change the tickets to leave from San Francisco instead of Los Angeles.

Surprised, the cashier insisted, "We have never sold those tickets here!"

You can believe it or not, but we are just simple enough to believe that God created those tickets just for us, because it was part of our destiny!

"Washington for Jesus," a huge demonstration at the White House mall in Washington D.C. was scheduled after we would leave, and we had tickets to go. It was hard for me to give it up, but we gave the tickets to C.L. and Candy Preston. "Pres" is the one who had visited us in Brazil. Also our son, Grant, went, so he represented our family.

We Join the Crew

"Honolulu, here we come!" It was interesting to see the type of people who took the promotional flight with us.

"This is a circus!" murmured our brother-in-law Bill, as he looked around the airport waiting room where he and Millie's sister Dorothy had come to see us off. One rotund young man was dancing in the waiting room wearing a luka, which is a man's sarong. Many seemed to be street people looking for a warmer climate. When we arrived the captain, a retired Coastguardsman showed us our cabin, apologizing for the bunk beds.

He and his wife were quite friendly, darkly tanned by constant exposure to the sun, about our ages. Claude turned 50 a few weeks later, and Millie was 47. They were glad to have us come as replacements for two young men who had left the crew. They were anxious to be on their way to Micronesia.

Four young men in their twenties completed the crew. Frank Lindley and Tom Kallander were the two *Haoles*, the Hawaiian word that jokingly describes white men from the mainland. Frank had been a vagabond surfer traveling the country in search of the biggest and best waves. Then he discovered the thrill of serving God was even greater, and gave him a life with a purpose. Calvin, of Philippine extraction, was born in Hawaii, and so was Wayne Yamamoto, a Japanese native Hawaiian.

"The boys are taking the ham radio license exam this morning," the captain said. "Someone on the crew needs to have a license so we can communicate with home."

We sat in the main salon waiting to hear the results. The inflatable dingy arrived, bringing them from shore.

"I failed," announced the first one to come down the companionway. The next two, without any emotion, also said they had failed.

The last one to enter was Frank. "I passed," he reported, being careful that his voice did not inflect any pride at the others' expense.

There were adjustments necessary for everyone when we joined the crew. The captain and his wife had been the leaders of six young men on the maiden voyage, when they brought the boat home from New Zealand. They had weathered some trials together, such as passing through the "doldrums." This is the section of the Pacific where there is very little wind.

The kerosene stove presented a challenge. Before it would light, one had to squirt a little alcohol in a trough to preheat the burner. No one was able to do this on a regular basis, and they ended up eating cold canned food for the last part of the trip. They all began to long to sink their teeth into a "Big Mac." The church, learning of their craving, met them when they arrived, bringing MacDonalds hamburgers for the whole crew.

The petite blonde captain's wife had been leading morning devotional meetings where any relationship issues were tackled, and it was a difficult thing for them to let us take that over, but we were asked to go as spiritual leaders, and that was our responsibility.

They both openly reacted negatively to our first attempt to lead. After a fruitless attempt to talk with them about it we made an appointment with the assistant pastor. What he told us was that on trial trips to other islands in the Hawaiian chain the captain, a fairly new convert, would go ashore and get drunk. This would make his wife nervous, and she would start smoking again.

A dark cloud descended over our spirits. We both felt a deep foreboding over the one year commitment ahead of us. Deciding that it was spiritual warfare, and we would have to fight through in prayer, we called our church at home to pray with us, and strengthened our resolve to go ahead with the trip.

People from the Honolulu church crowded the dock for a traditional Hawaiian sendoff. Many brought leis, standing in line to place them around our necks. Some leis were orchids and other flowers, others were made of gum and candies and others of Asian sweet and sour confections. The church school's elementary school children brought leis they had made from paper flowers and drinking straws.

The crew on the dock, left to right: Frank, Captain and wife, Wayne, Tom, Calvin, Millie and Claude.

As we cast off the lines and the sails caught the wind, we threw the inedible leis overboard. If they return to shore, tradition says, we will return.

The captain had warned us that the first three days we would be getting our "sea legs," and no one would feel well, but as we got accustomed to the motion of the sea our bodies would adapt. There was a lot of motion both side to side and fore and aft in the trade winds, with constant swells. In these conditions it is necessary to hold onto something whether walking on the deck or down below.

It was May, 1980, when we left Honolulu. It is good that we left when we did, because hurricane season begins in June and continues through November. Our first destination was the island or Majuro in the Marshall chain, then we were to go to Ponape, Kosrae, and Truk, all islands separated by great expanses of ocean.

The Marshalls include 35 atolls including Bikini and Aniwetok. Majuro is located seven degrees north of the equator, within the 1200 nautical mile strip around the earth where hurricanes normally do not occur, even though big waves had washed over it a short time before, washing away many homes. The Red Cross had provided tents while houses were being built for those whose homes were destroyed.

We were going to have to steer manually all the way, since the Jacaranda had no autopilot. The four boys and I, Claude, took four hour watches 24 hours a day. At night two of us would be on watch together.

Most of my sailing experience was with boats steered by a tiller attached directly to the rudder. The Jacaranda had a wheel and hydraulic steering, so that I could not feel the pressure on the rudder. The huge swells constantly threw us off course, since the wind was coming from behind.

"How close do we have to hold our course?" I asked the captain.

"Ten degrees," he said.

I thought to myself, "I don't think I can hold 15 degrees in these swells, let alone 10!"

The stress took its toll and I got a very painful stiff neck. One morning the captain's wife came into the cockpit with a jar of Vapor Rub and massaged my neck. It must have been God answering prayers, because the pain left immediately, and never came back.

Before we left on the trip I, Millie, prayed, "God, this is your destiny for us, please don't let me get seasick!"

It was a lot to ask, because I had a tendency towards motion sickness. God answered my prayer, although there were a few exceptions, like the day we caught a fish. Some was grilled, and some, known as *poki*, was a Korean recipe. Cubes of raw fish were marinated in soy sauce and garlic. Just to prove I was a good missionary, I took a second helping of *poki*. It was too much for a *haole*, and I soon was feeding the fish. That was humbling.

Claude, however, has never been seasick. His first ocean voyage was at the age of two weeks, when his parents brought him back to the United States from Manila, in the Philippine Islands where he was born.

"Claude and I were the only ones aboard to go to the dining room for meals," his father used to say. "All the other passengers were sick!"

Soon the eight of us were accustomed to life aboard. Our water supply was limited to what we carried in the water tanks had to be conserved. Out in the deep ocean sea water is clean, and it was used for bathing and washing dishes. When we wanted a bath we would drop a bucket over the side of the moving boat, tied to a rope. We used detergent rather than soap, since it worked better in salt water.

Three meals a day were prepared in the small galley and served outside in the cockpit. The cook had to compensate for the constant motion by using slide proof mats. The stove was on gimbals to keep it steady.

Every day at noon Frank and the captain would go on the foredeck, each having a sextant to take a shot of the sun to locate our position on the navigational chart. After two weeks we expected to see land.

"First one to sight land will get a prize," the captain's wife announced.

While Claude and I were on watch that afternoon we sighted palm trees on a flat island straight ahead.

"Land ho!" we shouted, and won a box of chocolate covered macadamia nuts.

The captain grimaced. "It's land," he agreed, "but not the right island."

There were always two troll lines dragging behind the boat, and the boys ran for the net when two beautiful fish, a barracuda and a yellow fin tuna took the lures. Later we caught many more.

"Sashimi tonight!" was the cry that went up every time we caught fish. Hawaiians are fond of this dish, thin slices of raw fish dipped in soy sauce flavored with Chinese mustard.

As we drew closer to Majuro we entered into hostile territory, and spiritual forces began to fight against us. First the wind stopped. We went under power, but the engine quit. Doubts arose among the crew as to whether or not we knew where we were.

We called a prayer meeting one evening to combat the problems. The captain, however, did not come out of his room. as he was a relatively new convert, he was offended to think we needed to pray rather than trust his leadership. Apparently he thought that by praying we were questioning his navigational skills. Nevertheless, things improved.

While I was praying about the engine problem, the Lord gave me the word, "Fuel injection pump."

Tom was good at mechanical problems, and he was checking the engine.

"The Lord told me its the fuel injection pump," I said.

"That was what I was thinking it is," he affirmed.

We had to wait until we got there to order a new part. In the meantime we were totally dependent on the wind, and there was not much of that.

"Praise the Lord, We Arrived!" Claude

We neared the entrance of Majuro lagoon during an early morning watch when Tom and I encountered a buoy.

"Let's set a reverse course and tack back and forth here by the buoy, and we will be ready to head in when the captain wakes up," I suggested, and that was what we did.

It took 12 hours to cover the relatively short distance because there was very little wind. We set the anchor and praised the

Lord. We made it! It had taken 18 days at sea to arrive at our first destination.

Going ashore, Tom ordered a new fuel pump. It was being shipped from Honolulu, and barges only arrived from there once a month. Also stress had built up in our relationship with the captain and his wife.

The captain began going ashore and getting drunk. He did not drink privately, but drew attention to himself by being rowdy in the bars. This was a poor representation of Jesus to the people on the island. Predictably, his wife started smoking again.

I had to be the bad guy and contact the church to tell them. The pastor from Hawaii made a trip to visit us and settle the problem. His decision was to send the other couple home. Frank was appointed as captain and Tom as first mate.

One evening when everyone else had gone ashore, we stayed aboard with Frank, who was on watch. A storm whipped up the wind, blowing us towards shore.

"I'm afraid we might drag anchor!" Frank said in alarm. "The boat might be damaged, because there are coral reefs between where we are and the shore."

"Frank," Claude said, "This is the kind of situation where we need to do what Jesus did on the Sea of Galilee, when a storm came up. He commanded the wind to be still."

"That wouldn't be right!" Frank insisted. "God is the one who sends the wind and controls the weather, we don't!"

He left us in the salon and began pacing up and down the deck. We stayed below and prayed, rebuking the storm. Then we went to bed, and in the morning it was calm.

"What happened last night?" Claude asked Frank, smiling inwardly.

A little shame faced he answered, "I got mad, and I marched up to the stern and shook my fist and told the wind to stop in the name of Jesus!"

"Then what happened?"

"The wind stopped."

God has a way of humbling us.

When the new fuel injector arrived, Tom repaired the engine. Our instructions were not to stay long in the Marshalls, because there had been a lot of Christian missionaries there already, but go on to make contacts in other islands of Micronesia. We could not leave, however, because Frank had not learned enough about navigation.

Pastor Samuel, of the Assembly of God Church, took a liking to us, and invited us to move the boat to anchor near the church, saying we could use the showers in the church's rustic restroom. There, the roaches the size of horses lived. He asked Claude to teach an adult Sunday School class and the boys to lead midweek youth meetings. Frank and Tom were each given a Sunday morning to preach.

Wayne Yamamoto was an immediate hit with the younger children, when they found out he had a black belt in Karate. His real passion, however, was in the area of health. He had come prepared with a small first aid kit. Kids would come to him with their scratches and bruises, and he would treat them. As soon as he went ashore the children would all run after him.

Wayne applies antiseptic to an "owie."

"Rachael, this is for your sore throat," he would say, and give her a dose of cough medicine.

"Lucia, you need drops for your eyes," as she lifted her trusting face.

"George, let me see your knee.

Then he went to a tent where he told the parents, "I'm here to take care of Billy's toenail."

"Oh, but he's asleep," they replied.

"That's even better," and he took out a pair of scissors to operate on a loose toenail.

"You're a good doctor!" said the father.

All the four boys picked up enough of the language to carry on animated conversations with the young people. Most people spoke English too, but the native language was used in Church meetings. Otherwise, someone would interpret.

Yokwe, was like *Aloha* in Hawaiian, doubling for hello, goodbye, and love. Strangely, *ehno* (pronounced like "no") means good.

As the boys took turns teaching the youth group, Calvin had them laughing, telling how he was overly concerned about getting freshwater showers, but the Lord taught him a lesson.

One time he was in the shower, lathered up, shampoo on the hair, when the water was shut off. There was a water shortage on the island, and it only ran two hours a day.

Frank taught the youth the Bible way of worship, not only singing songs we know, but spontaneous group singing given by the Spirit. He was surprised that as soon as he stopped speaking they began singing like a chorus of angels as they were inspired by the Holy Spirit. It is so natural for Marshallese to sing. It is a major part of their culture. It was also natural for them to trust God and receive all He has for them.

We went to the clinic to pray for patients.

"You should come pray for Manasseh. He is suffering from high blood pressure. He may have had a stroke," someone told Claude.

He went into a room where Manasseh, a local dentist, occupied a bed.

"God loves you, and he wants to give you peace and to heal your body," Claude said.

We prayed for him, and the next day his blood pressure was normal and he was sent home. He had never gone to church before, but he started going to every service. His wife saw a change in him, and she began reading the Bible and going to church with him.

Millie had to go to the clinic for an infection, and while I, Claude, was waiting for her a man in a hospital gown walked up to me as I leaned against the building. His eyes had a wild look about them.

"Will you pray for me to be delivered?" he asked.

"Yes, I will pray for you, but first you need to ask Jesus to come into your heart," I responded.

I led him in a prayer, then asked God to deliver him.

Weeks later a group of young people ran up as I arrived in the dingy.

"There is a man looking for you!" they exclaimed.

Following them, I discovered it was the man I had prayed for at the clinic. His eyes had lost the wild look.

"Do you remember me?" he asked. "I'm Theodore. You prayed for me, and now I am delivered!"

After he left the young people told me he had been a lunatic, and even tried to kill a man.

Micronesia was under the United Nations, and the Marshalls were a protectorate of the United States. It had been 25 years since we were inspired by reading about the man who sailed to the Marshalls to protest the atom bomb testing at Bikini atoll.

We found that the population of Bikini had been relocated to Kili. They could not return to their native island because radioactivity still infected food grown there, including the fish. They are still living on Kili, 65 years following the test.

We got acquainted with the senator who represented Bikini in the United States Congress.

"I am going on an inter island trip to visit the residents of Bikini next week," he told us. "You can go along, if you like. I'm sorry I cannot give you a cabin, but you can sleep with the passengers on the deck and eat with the other Americans."

A major problem with the people living on Kili was that it had no lagoon. At Bikini the lagoon had been teeming with fish. The inter island boat had to anchor offshore, and passengers were ferried to the island in a small boat.

We joined with many of the older Bikini residents for a meeting with lawyers, representatives, and salesmen for solar cells to generate electricity. The meeting began with the people singing a song about their home island, weeping as they sang. The sacrifice that they were asked to make, "for the good of mankind," was more than they were prepared for.

Afterwards we walked through the village of simple wooden homes. One of the benefits that the United States gave them was freezers in their homes, something that only wealthy people could own in Majuro.

We tried to talk with a group of young people sitting on a set of rusty bedsprings.

They couldn't speak English, but when we sang a Christian song, they brightened up, and responded by singing the same song in their language. Their mother came out of the house and gave us a sample of native handcraft, a fan made of fiber from the trunk of the coconut palms that now decorates a wall in our study.

"I bring food from afar," Millie

I was almost totally involved in cooking for the crew. There was one supermarket in town where I bought the groceries every day, since our refrigerator quit working before we arrived. Once during our morning devotions Tom paid me a compliment.

"Millie is like the virtuous woman in Proverbs 31," he said, "She brings food from afar."

Tom took charge of assigning tasks to each crew member to maintain the boat. Claude's job was varnishing the teak woodwork, and mine was mending sail covers.

Tom, the young first mate, also had a great sense of humor and of drama.

One morning he hollered, "I want the crew to assemble for the Captain's inspection!"

Wayne and Calvin and I fell into line in front of Tom, who gave Frank a snappy salute. "The crew is ready for inspection sir!"

Then he looked around, "Except for Seaman Claude, where is Seaman Claude?"

"He's in the head," responded Wayne," whereupon Tom turned to Frank, and with a salute, pulled in his chin saying stuffily, "He's doing his duty, sir!"

"I feel like I need a vacation. Do you mind if I take an inter island trip?" Frank asked. "A boat is leaving to visit several islands. I would be gone for ten days."

"Of course, you need a break," Claude agreed.

He boarded a ship that was going to stop at several islands. While he was aboard he met the captain.

"I need to learn to navigate," he said, explaining that our captain unexpectedly had to leave.

The friendly Marshallese captain took him in hand and taught him navigation. The inter island trip stretched from 10 days to two weeks, extending the time Frank could be instructed. When he returned he was ready to navigate, and we would be able to complete our trip.

Passengers had to supply their own food on the inter island boats, so Frank had brought along some nonperishable foods from the Super Market.

"I made friends with some guys, and we all shared our food. My food disappeared in a few days," he said, "but one of the Marshallese guys worked in the galley.

"After every meal he brought out the leftover rice and meat and we all shared it. The last day he poured the food out on a newspaper for us to eat with our fingers, like we usually did, but I almost gagged. I guess culture shock caught up with me."

Now it was possible for us to travel to other islands. Tony, assistant pastor of the Assembly of God church in Majuro, suggested we visit a neighboring island, Arno. There was a church there that had no pastor. Tony went along with us. It was an easy sail, but everyone had to regain their sea legs

The first people to greet us were the children, who gathered around Tom and Frank, who had brought their guitars. They were still weak from the first passage in months, and barely whispered the words to the songs. The kids didn't mind, but bent close to hear.

As we walked down the path, passing the houses along the way, Tony announced that there would be prayer for healing at the church in the morning.

Wayne and Calvin volunteered to have a meeting for the children that evening. Wayne's parents were Buddhists, but he accepted Christ as a child in a neighborhood Children's' Bible Club.

"What shall I do?" he asked Claude.

"Do you remember what the woman did when you first accepted the Lord as a child? Just do the same thing," Claude suggested.

Wayne took a flannel board and pictures of the life of Christ. When they returned to the boat after the meeting, he was jubilant.

"All thirty children accepted Christ tonight!" he reported.

Everyone on the island must have attended the morning service. After the benches were full, they sat on mats in the back. Millie and Claude taught on healing and deliverance, and Tony preached. Then we prayed for the sick.

The Church in Honolulu sent Captain Kres Ketchem, a Canadian who had sailed missionary boats among islands of the Pacific, to teach us the rudiments of sailing among coral reefs.

He and a Congregational missionary went along with us and we sailed to a Christian high school in Rong Rong, an island across the lagoon from Majuro. A Youth With a Mission team of young men went along, bringing the Jesus film based on the book of Luke. The film was projected on our sail, and the projector run by the boat generator. Island people came alongside in whatever boats they had. They were deeply moved as they watched the life of Christ.

"Do you have any breadfruit I could have?" Millie asked the high school principal.

His eyes lit up, "Tomorrow we will bring lunch to your boat."

The next day some of the ladies came out bearing breadfruit soup, French fried breadfruit, breadfruit salad, boiled breadfruit and breadfruit 'cheese,' all the resourceful ways it could be prepared.

"I was so sorry that we did not know in advance you were coming. We didn't have much food on hand," the principal said, "But we had lots of breadfruit!"

Tarawa, an island stronghold of the Japanese during World War II, was our next destination. Several young teenage boys sitting on a wharf caught my attention. Since arriving in the islands, I had not seen teenagers look so calloused. As we tied up to the dock I silently prayed that God would set them free from the mocking spirit.

One of the residents took us to the beach and showed us Japanese artillery guns.

Her grandfather, Claude, was a German missionary to the Marshall Islands.

Pointing to a structure nearby he explained, "That is where they beheaded our people if they were caught taking more than one coconut a day for food."'

A young lady who spoke good English invited us to come into her simple thatched house. She explained she had gone to high school in Oregon.

"I saw your boat coming into the island, and you were working very hard," she said. I thought, "They must really love us, to work that hard to get here!' What are your names?"

"Claude!", she exclaimed. "My grandfather's name was Claude. He was a German missionary."

She took us to see the remains of Japanese Zero fighter planes almost hidden by tropical foliage.

"There is another American who came with the Peace Corps. Now he lives here, but he is not good. He taught the boys to smoke marihuana. He sits cross legged and worships the sun!"

I remembered the boys I saw on the wharf. Frank encountered the man she spoke of. "Nothing he said made sense," Frank commented.

"I'm writing a book about UFOs," he told them.

There was no pastor for the church in Tarawa. On Sunday we held a service in the bombed out remains of the Japanese communications building. The UFO author interpreted the message. We were all praying for him, and he did an excellent job.

Trying Times Begin

Each week Claude would meet with Pastor Samuel and check with him to make sure he approved of the lesson for the week. This went well until the American missionary administrator for the denomination came down from Kwajilan Island.

"Your group is here to win the souls of the people and take them out of our church and start your own church," he insisted.

Claude assured him that was not the case, but he replied, "You are not licensed by our denomination, and are not permitted to minister in our churches."

As though that were not enough, we got news that there had been a scandal in the home church in Honolulu that affected all the ministries of the church. The pastor left his wife for a young lady.

On top of that we found out through our ham radio communications that my 90 year old mother had been hospitalized with pneumonia.

There was an airport on Majuro, and I could have gone home to be with my mother, but because I felt sure it was God's will for me to stay and finish the year, since it was only four more months, I just prayed God would keep her alive until I arrived. Still, I was very stressed. No matter what I did I had a heavy feeling of depression.

My birthday came in March, but I was not happy about that. When some of the island girls found out I was depressed they arrived at the boat bringing a gift, a beautiful heart shaped basket made by their mother of palm fibers.

A wealthy man had invited the crew to eat at his home that evening. When he found out it was my birthday he brought a cake out of the freezer, apologizing that the inscription was, "Happy Birthday Margaret."

"It was made for a girl who left before we could give it to her," he explained.

We had received bad news about Ponape. The government had notified the church they would not allow us to go there because of a policy against new churches.

My concern for the mission added to the tension I felt.

"Claude," I said, "I am going into the cabin. I feel like I need to cry."

I went there and began to cry loudly, but after a few minutes everything that had happened to prevent us from leaving Majuro looked funny in my mind. Although I intended to cry it out, I began to laugh.

Frank and Claude heard me from the salon. They looked at each other in surprise.

"I can't understand these *wahines*!" exclaimed Frank, as they stared at each other and laughed. *Wahine* is Hawaiian for women.

So God broke through my depression and gave me joy from the Lord.

I was thankful that God set me free from tension before Wayne became sick. His temperature climbed to 104 degrees, then 106. He lay on the salon floor, weakened, while I sponged his arms and legs with tepid water.

The doctor at the Majuro clinic could not diagnose it for three days. When the whites of Wayne's eyes turned yellow it was apparent he had hepatitis, and must fly back to Honolulu for treatment. He and Calvin had eaten some raw shellfish they found on the other side of the island, thinking that it would be harmless on the ocean side.

Although hepatitis is highly contagious, no one else caught it while we were in Majuro. Wayne recovered at home in Hawaii. The last we heard, he and his wife were missionaries to Japan.

We prepared the leave, and the church had a going away party. As was their custom, the women made matching shirts and muumuus for us and some other missionaries to wear.

"When the first missionaries arrived at our islands in 1860," said the speaker, "our forefathers had to decide whether to eat them or listen to what they had to say. They listened, and that is why we have come to know God today."

Manasseh came to where Claude was seated and spoke of him, "If this man had not come here, I would not be a believer today, but my life completely changed after he prayed for me at the clinic."

Our departure was delayed for another month while we cleaned and painted the Jacaranda's hull, but on the morning we were to leave, some people gathered at the church to give us gifts and bid us a final farewell.

"See this?" said little Antonio, pointing to a barely visible scar, "Wayne healed that!" It was sad to leave such a wonderful place. They sent us off with a branch of bananas, sack of coconuts, and breadfruit.

Our Trip to Guam, Claude

On the trip to Guam Calvin began to have symptoms of hepatitis. Being raised in Hawaii, the only thing he felt like eating was sashimi. He lay on the deck, dipping the raw fish in soy sauce and mustard.

Rather than staying in his bunk, he stretched out on the floor of the Salon, the same as Wayne had done when he was sick. He flew back to Honolulu from Guam with us when we left for home.

It was beautiful steering the boat at night in the tropics, wearing cutoffs, a shirt and being barefooted. Rather than watch the compass I, would set the course by the compass, then pick a star on course and keep my eye on that.

We always conserved water, so it was a treat when we went through a thunder storm and we could quickly take a fresh water shower in the rain. But it took Millie too long to put on a bathing suit, and she missed out.

"Do you mind if I use a bucket of fresh water for a shower?" she asked Frank.

But he refused. Just to get even she lowered a bucket into the ocean and poured it over his head from behind while he was at the wheel.

"Millie! I just took a fresh water shower!" he exclaimed.

"I know, but you won't let me take one," she retorted, and everyone laughed.

Frank did a good job of navigation.

"Land Ho!" someone yelled. It was Guam. We had covered 1600 nautical miles, and it took two weeks. We had covered 1800 nautical miles coming from Honolulu to Majuro, and it took 21 days.

Grace Bible in Honolulu started a church in Guam that took us in. The people were great at going to the microphone to report encouraging words God was saying. Often a child would give a word to encourage someone.

When we arrived at Guam, we were given a letter from our church at home saying that my position on the church staff had been filled while I was gone.

"We will pray for your future ministry," Ernest wrote. I may have brought this about myself by assigning the jobs I did to volunteers.

Calvin flew back to Honolulu along with us, where we caught our flight home. Tom and Frank were joined by the two young men who had been on the boat to bring it to Hawaii from New Zealand after the church bought it. From Guam they sailed safely back to the home port.

Since the pastor who had the vision for the boat ministry had left the church in Honolulu, the assistant pastor took over. It was decided to sell the boat and give the proceeds to Youth With a Mission for their boat ministry.

"While we were out on the Jacaranda," I told Millie, "God told me that he would give us a boat of our own."

I thought of eventually having a team of sailboats with individual couples on each boat. They then could be dispatched to different islands, meeting from time to time at a central location.

I presented the idea to the church, but after considering it, they decided they could not support us this time.

God took one away, but added one to our family. Millie

Before we left for Honolulu the year before I had told Scott and Grant, who were in their 20s, "Grandma is 89 years old, and anything could happen while we are gone. I am leaving her in your hands. Please watch out for her."

They agreed that they would, and they had done very well with very little contact with me. They visited her regularly at the senior housing apartment where she lived.

When she got sick the housing office phoned Laurie, Scott's wife, to say that one of the tenants met their grandmother in the hall, and that she was wheezing badly, breathing with difficulty. Scott and Laurie took her to the hospital, where she was diagnosed with pneumonia. They made a schedule so that one of them, Scott, Laurie, or Grant visited her every day. They celebrated her ninetieth birthday in her hospital room.

When she recovered, it was advised she be placed in a nursing home. Scott, Laurie and Grant visited many homes until they found the best one, and that is where I found her when we arrived.

"You are my apple blossom baby!" she exclaimed when she realized I was not just another of the nursing personnel.

It was then I remembered I had sent her the only get well card I could find in Majuro with a picture of apple blossoms on it. When I bought it I did not realize she used to call me her apple blossom baby and that she would make that association!

My Jesus had kept her alive in answer to my prayers, and I was near her for six weeks. She recommitted her soul to Jesus before she went to be with Him a few months later.

We had received a letter from Grant while we were in Majuro with some good news.

"You know how Debbie Radcliff and I were 'Just friends?'" he wrote, "Well, we are more than friends now, we are going to get married!"

No sooner had we lost my mother than we gained a new family member, another daughter-in-law. Debbie was a delightful addition to the family, a fun loving, stimulating person. Both our daughters-in-law are good home makers and mothers. Laurie did the bookkeeping for Scott's contracting business and home schooled their boys at times, preferring to stay home and be an attentive mom over working outside the home.

On March 25, 1982, our first grandchild was born to Scott and Laurie. They named him Andrew Scott. Claude's Grandfather

Roderick Kerr was a great help to him when his parents were divorced, and it was a wonderful blessing to him to become a grandfather.

As we laid in bed that night after we saw Andrew for the first time at the hospital Claude marveled, "I just can't get that little baby's face out of my mind!"

CHAPTER SIX

Death and Resurrection of the Vision

We Sell Everything *Again,* Millie
Soon after God had called me to go to foreign lands Jesus spoke to me as he did to a rich young man from the ruling class:
"You still lack one thing. Sell all that you have and distribute to the poor, and you will have treasure in heaven; and come, follow Me." Luke 18:22

We came back to that place again when we returned to the States. After unsuccessfully searching for work for a time, we discovered that we were in the middle of a recession that began while we were gone.

One evening we sat forlornly in our home, wondering how in the world we could realize our dream of having our own boat for missionary work.

"Do you have any ideas?" Claude asked me.

"We can sell everything," I said. It just popped out. Jesus told the rich young man to sell everything, "and come follow me."

"Lets sell this house, and rent an apartment. We can sell both our cars and buy cheaper ones." Claude answered.

From then on God's blessings began to be poured out on us. If we hadn't known Jesus or never read the Bible we would have thought we had "good luck," but throughout our lives we have learned it is God's blessing.

Another way God blessed us was with wisdom. Claude makes it a practice to read a chapter from the book of Proverbs, the Bible's section on wisdom, every day. In Proverbs we found principles on how to make money and handle finances

This is how we did it, Claude.

We sold our cars, bought cheaper ones, and moved into a studio apartment So it was job hunting time. Several things were against me. The country was in the middle of recession when we arrived in 1981. Also, I had been out of the surveying field for 11 years. There was new equipment that I had no experience using. I applied for positions but nothing was available. One job I applied for had 100 applicants competing for only one opening.

I finally got a job painting with a crew contracted to Ford Aerospace. The foreman, Gene, was Christian believer like me.

"You really know how to handle that brush!" he said as he watched me varnishing some cabinets.

"I did a lot of varnishing aboard a boat," I explained.

Gene and I became great friends. Once we were both up on high ladders painting a ceiling in a vacant room, both of us singing praise songs at the top of our lungs.

"I thank God for sending you here, I needed your friendship to get through life right now," he said.

"And you are a real blessing to me!" I replied.

After about a year I got a job as map checker for Redwood City. It was rough working for my boss, and I disliked desk jobs, but stuck it out until there was an opening in the town of Los Gatos. A party chief position opened with the water district. I got the job, but after a short time I discovered the crew were all resentful of me because each of them felt he should have gotten the job instead of me.

It was useless trying to head up that crew. They just were not cooperating. I told my supervisor I was resigning.

"When?" he asked.

"Yesterday!" I answered.

He knew the situation I had been in, and understood.

At that point I wasn't eager to get another job right away. I was completely burned out. However, driving down the street one day I saw a county survey crew that I knew. They told me about an opening for an instrument man.

It was 1984. I applied, took the test, and was called for an interview. I walked in and saw some of the men who I had worked with in previous years waiting to interview me.

"I'm not familiar with the new equipment," I warned them.

"You are willing to learn, aren't you?" said one of my old buddies.

I was willing, and got the job. It was such a relief to be happy with my work, after four years of frustration.

Our Family Grows, Millie

From that time on our family grew rapidly. Grant and Debbie's first child, Alex, was born in September, 1984. Two weeks later, Scott and Laurie had another boy, Brandon.

Debbie complained, "You don't have a chance of having a girl in the Kerr family!"

That seemed to be so. We had two boys, and now our two sons had three boys.

In 1987, when Debbie was pregnant again Claude was moved to pray, "Lord, if you really want to bless me, give me a granddaughter!"

The ultrasound was not invented yet, so when we went to the hospital and saw our first granddaughter, Alisha Diane, Claude began to weep for joy!

He kept saying, "I just can't get over how much God loves me!"

Apparently God wanted to demonstrate his love even more, because 14 months later Grant and Debbie had another girl, Lauren Rene Kerr!

Claude tells about buying a house

A friend had a rental house that was going to be repossessed.

I paid him $1,000 and took over the payments. It was better for him to get something out of it, and to save his credit rating.

We moved out of the apartment and into the house, just after the renters had left. The roof leaked and the sheetrock was falling off the walls. The carpet was worn completely through to the floor in spots. It was the worst house on the street.

We went to work weekends and evenings, tearing out the carpet, ripping off outmoded wallpaper, painting inside and out, and spraying big black beetles that came out at night. Our son Scott got rid of a valley in the roof, thus stopping the leak.

In one year we changed that house from the worst to the best on the block. Even so, it was not a good neighborhood. Next door was a drug addict who beat up his girlfriend when she suggested he get into a rehab program.

So we asked our friend, Preston, to sell the house for us. He found a customer immediately, and we signed the papers. As it turned out, we made more money that year on the house than I did working all year on my job. We asked Pres to help us find another house. One day he phoned.

"I found you a house you will love! It's in The Villages, a senior complex in the foothills."

As he drove us into the grounds we entered a gate past the security guards.

The Villages had 300 acres, hiking trails, swimming pools and much more. Wow! What a place in the edges of a busy city. We liked it, so we bought a two bedroom two bath townhouse. Even the landscaping was taken care of, so I didn't have to keep it up myself.

"This is the best house you have had!" exclaimed our daughter-in-law, Debbie. "I like coming here to visit."

We had many family dinners there. It was a great place for entertaining or going for a picnic. We could walk, swim, and hike, and the security guards patrolled nightly.

In 1985 Scott and Laurie decided to move to Omaha. The Holy Spirit spoke to each of them separately before they discussed it. Laurie's parents lived there, and they were able to better their lives. We missed them all greatly. We began to make it a habit to visit them twice a year to keep up with the rapid growth of the boys. It was not long when Scott phoned.

"I bought a house!" he exclaimed. It was one hundred years old, and needed a lot of work. He is not afraid of work, and turned it into a lovely home.

We were very content. Work was going well for both of us, and Naomi was working as a substitute teacher. I started paying back my retirement fund that I had taken out when we first went to Brazil. We also saved a large part of my paycheck in a tax free savings fund.

From 1981, when I lost the job at the church until 1989, in just eight years, because we had a vision for our lives, we moved from owing $1100 a month more than our income to retiring. Without a vision you die, the Bible says. (Proverbs 29:18) God will help us fulfill his will in our lives if we make him our priority and seek his will for us.

We Buy Destiny!

I found out the hard way that it might take a little time, but will happen, if we remain faithful. It was hard for me, because I didn't start at a younger age, but some of you who are reading this will be able to begin sooner. God has a plan for all of us!

We still had the same plan to sail out and help this messed up world. We began to seriously look at boats. For one reason or another, most boats didn't appeal to me

I wanted a boat that was easy to sail and not too big. It should be one that could be sailed single-handed, by either myself or Naomi, in an emergency, and of course, one we could afford. But, above everything else, we wanted one that was strong and seaworthy.

One day I was looking at a Cruising World magazine, and saw one advertised that had only one sail, a cat rig, sailors call it. I said to myself, "I know how to sail that! I used to race El Toros. They are catboats." We checked out this boat further, and decided it was what we wanted. It was a 30-foot Nonsuch. I got to meet the Canadian architect who designed it, as well as the builder. The Nonsuch was fast, exceptionally easy to sail, and the accommodations were good. She had plenty of storage for water, fuel, and provisions.

We found a used, classic model in good shape. She would help fulfill the destiny God had for our lives, so "Destiny" was her new name! Remember, God has a destiny for you, too. It may not have anything to do with boats, because he didn't create us all the same. Yours will be tailor made for you!

We bought a 30-foot, cat rigged Nonsuch and named her Destiny.

Jesus said, "Come to me, all of you who are weary and carry heavy burdens, and I will give you rest...For my yoke fits perfectly, and the burden I give you is light!" (Matthew 11:28,30 NLB) So, we just have to seek him, and commit ourselves to him, in order to see it happen in our lives. Trust me, I found He is faithful to make our dreams come true.

We brought *Destiny* back to Redwood City, just down the Bay from San Jose. After living in The Villages for two years, we were well rested and happy to sell the townhouse, sell or give away everything unnecessary, and store a few things in the same steamer trunks we used to move to Brazil. We stored them in a loft in Grant's garage that had a pull-down ladder for access. Then we loaded our clothes, miniature sewing machine, portable typewriter, and supplies onto the Destiny at the Marina, which would be our home base for the next three years.

It was Christmas Eve, 1985, that we moved onto our boat. A group of neighbors who lived aboard boats in the marina were our first visitors. They stood on the dock where we were berthed and serenaded us with Christmas Carols. That was our first experience with the boating community.

Instead of paying a house mortgage or rent, we only had a small loan to pay off the boat and a reasonable berth fee. We actually saved over $30,000 in living expenses by living on our boat those years. During that time we got to know our boat inside and out.

We brought along a bird cage, the home of Dr. Pepper, a perky little cockatiel who filled the empty nest when the boys got married. This amazing bird talked to us. "Dr. Pepper" were his first words, but he soon picked up a 30 word vocabulary. He quickly learned to imitate his new neighbors, the seagulls. Naomi often took him with her to visit her classes. I was very content working as an instrument man for Santa Clara County. The party chief was Tom Ballard, a Christian believer. Instead of the hectic work I had done before, surveying for freeways, we were assigned to jobs in the hills, close to nature.

The county announced an opening for party chief, but I didn't apply. I was getting ready to retire in another year, and didn't feel right about quitting after only one year, forcing the county to go through the hiring procedure again.

"Why didn't you apply for the party chief job?" my supervisor asked me the next day.

"I'm planning on retiring soon," I answered.

"Wouldn't you like to make more money?" he asked.

"Sure."

He slapped me on the shoulder. "Go ahead and apply!"

I did apply, and got the job. This was the same position I had worked at 17 years earlier. It had taken me six years to gradually work up to my old position I held when I quit to go to Brazil. God is faithful. The Bible says that when a man pleases God, He makes even his enemies become his friends. He does what his Word, the Bible, says. All we have to do is believe, and ask. He says, "Ask, and you will receive!"

Millie Continues, Back to China

In 1986 China was wide open for foreign travel. Forward Edge, an organization that grew out of the Gospel Outreach Church, announced an opportunity to join a short term team. They would be sent to evangelize in China. Our hearts were stirred, and we signed up to go. It was scheduled for three weeks in October.

However, when school opened in September I had a long term assignment teaching a 6th grade class in a Junior High School. The vice principal said they were considering giving me a contract. I was very interested. It was an opportunity to double my income, and I wanted to help pay off our loan and to outfit Destiny. We notified Bob Bergeron, the team captain, that we would not be able to go.

Shortly after that a check arrived in the mail. It was nearly enough for my expenses, from an anonymous donor in Alaska, where Bob lived. It was hard for me to give up the prospect of a contract for the year, but I finally decided to go.

The team gathered in Hong Kong. Along with us, there were eight people from all over the United States. At that time Bibles were still very scarce in China. The first week of our mission was spent taking Bibles over the border.

"They won't do anything to you if you are caught," our missionary friend told us, "because China wants tourists. they will only confiscate your Bibles."

This is not true of Chinese citizens. They have been executed for taking Bibles to the Christians who are eager to get them.

With the ten of us making trips across the border every day we were able to deliver hundreds of the small books, which included the Old and New Testaments. We simply prayed that God would make a way, and he always did.

As we prayed about our trip from Hong Kong to Beijing we were led to take a train from Canton to Wuhan. We would then board a boat on the Yangtze River headed for the famous Gorges. We carried several thousand illustrated tracts in our luggage, telling the main points of the gospel from Genesis to Revelation.

Since the trip was Spirit led, we had no reservations. For a day and a night we sat on hard benches on a train from Canton to Wuhan. A Chinese man who shared our bench smiled his "good night" and slid to the floor underneath the table that separated us from the seat across from us and went to sleep. Soon a man and woman who wanted to speak to us and practice their English arrived to occupy the seat he had vacated.

Before we boarded the boat we spent a day and night at a high rise hotel in Wuhan. Claude went out on the street in the morning

OUR DESTINY

with a camera to see the town. I stayed in the hotel room, many stories above the street. I was burdened to pray to know our future in China. I had heard that English teachers were wanted,

"Father, if you want me to come to China again and teach English, make it plain to me," I prayed.

While I was seeking God in prayer, I looked out the window, and saw a crowd forming far below on the sidewalk. Thinking of Claude, I prayed for his protection.

When he returned, Claude had quite a story to tell. The crowd I had seen was gathered to watch a man who was twisting a rod of iron rebar around his neck. It reminded me of the Brazilian town where priests and others walked on a bed of hot coals by the power of the devil.

Claude focused his camera on him. The man responded by coming towards him, not only with the twisted rod around his neck, but a twisted diabolic grimace on his face.

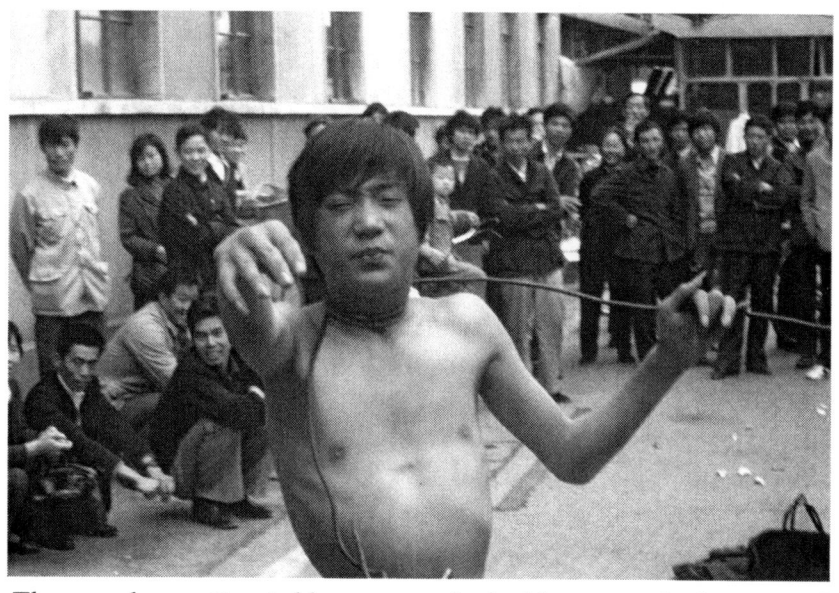

The crowd was attracted by a man who had bent a steel rebar around his neck by the power of Satan.

"He's mad because you didn't ask permission to take his picture," said a man standing next to Claude. "He wants you to pay him."

Reaching into his pocket, Claude took some money and handed it to the deranged man and made a hasty retreat.

We thanked God that Claude wasn't attacked! It was by divine providence that there was a man standing next to him who could speak English and knew what to do. Perhaps he was an angel!

After our sleepless night on the train, we were ten happy campers when we boarded the river boat and found out we each had a bunk in a large room all to ourselves. Guitars appeared, and we sang and worshipped in our appreciation to God. Curious faces appeared though the windows.

One of our teammates came from a GO church in Mendocino County, south of Humboldt County. Coming from a life far from God, he chose a new name, Mattole. He wore a cowboy hat and sported a graying beard and mustache.

Mattole and Claude waited outside the dining room when the doors were opened for the passengers to exit a Kung Fu movie. The throng mobbed them to get the tracts they offered. Then a steady stream began visiting our cabin, motioning they wanted Bibles, which we gave them. The next morning more asked for tracts and Bibles for themselves and others.

After we got back to Hong Kong we were told that it was not advised to give out tracts on the boats, due to heavy security, but God protected us.

In the morning when we went to the dining room for breakfast the waiter apologized that they had no American food for us, since we hadn't made reservations. So we had a Chinese breakfast. There were pickles made from tiny bulbs of seaweed along with other delicacies.

Judy Nettle, one of the young ladies on the team, bowed her head a little longer than the rest of us.

"I prayed before we came on this trip that I would be able to eat everything," she said. We all ate the food everywhere we went and enjoyed it without incident.

Many of the English speaking passengers were professors at a university in Wuhan. A woman professor asked me wistfully, "Is it true that in the United States women may live with a man without marrying him?"

"Many people do, but it is not God's way. I am a Christian believer, and I am very happy to be married to my husband for life!" I told her.

She invited me to her cabin, which had several bunk beds. As we talked a handsome young man in uniform came in and lay on a bunk and began to read.

"He shares my berth with me," she explained, tossing her head towards him with the same careless expression I had seen on the faces of other women in China.

"The government thinks it is enough for my husband and me to be together one week a year," she said disdainfully. "They assigned him to a job far away in North China."

I met another college professor, a man, who asked me if I had a college degree.

"What was your major?" he asked me.

"Journalism," I replied.

"We need English teachers in China. I will write you a letter of recommendation, if you would like to apply," he said

Back in our cabin I told Claude about it.

"When we were in Wuhan I asked God for to make it clear to me if he wanted me to return to China to teach English. I believe this is the answer."

"Maybe you should. But I couldn't teach English."

I tried to convince him he could, but he did not feel the same calling. I had to back down. God gave him the authority to make final decisions. *Genesis 3:16 and I Corinthians 11:3* A preacher once said, "If you don't hear from God on a subject, then go by principle." That is the principle I went by.

When we disembarked in Nanking and were waiting for transportation in a public plaza, three children came to us begging for money while their mother watched them, smiling. Seeing them, one of our women wept. Because she had more than two children, the government would not give the mother a job.

In Hong Kong our missionary friend had strongly advised us to attend an English speaking church in Beijing.

"I believe you will make a valuable contact there," he said.

What he said came true. A woman from Idaho stood up and said, "I am a pastor's wife from Sandpoint, Idaho. I teach English in a university in a Northern province. My students have taken a great interest in my religion. I came to Beijing to see if I could find Bibles to take to them."

We were wondering what to do with the satchel full of Bibles that remained. We turned them over to her. After we got home, we received a letter from her. She was able to direct her students to put on a Christmas pageant. Farmers brought animals and straw for the stable.

While we were in Beijing we visited Tiananmen Square. There was a huge picture of Mao Zedong there. I gave a few people tracts, but had to stop before I attracted the attention of the authorities.

We thought of passing out tracts on the great wall, and a fellow teammate quipped, "I can just see the headline in the next issue of the GO newsletter: **"Forward Edge Team, Off the Wall!"**

When it came time to fly back to Hong Kong to make connections for our flight home, we faced a huge problem. Bob had written to the mother of a Chinese student he had met at home, asking her to make reservations for the team, but she was unable to do it.

We told an American resident of Beijing about our dilemma.

He laughed. "You don't know how hard it is to get reservations! And ten on one flight? Impossible!"

Undaunted, we prayed about it. Claude felt we should go to a specific airlines office. He and Bob went to the ticket office while we sat down to a American breakfast of familiar foods at the hotel. We enjoyed our favorite cold cereals, yogurt, coffee, and juice. After all the things He had done for us, we all had confidence that God would not let us down.

Before we finished eating, they returned with ten tickets!

We went to the same hotel for lunch. Again, the menu featured American food, which we were ready for. Claude and I ordered hamburgers and apple pie a la mode. I went to the restroom, and gave the attendant a tract. While I was in the stall, I saw many feet going by, and heard excited conversations in Chinese.

"They are really excited about the story of Jesus!" I thought. "These Chinese are *so* ready for the gospel!"

We enjoyed the food immensely, but soon afterwards I asked Claude to pray for me. "I have horrible stomach cramps!" I said. He prayed, but they didn't go away immediately. Boarding the plane, and we sat in the front seats behind the first class section.

"We have two extra meals for first class. It's lobster. Would you like that?" the hostess asked us. "What luck! God is really blessing us!" I thought. But when she brought the food I was still suffering from stomach cramps, and had to turn it down.

God Gives Me a New Name

After we got home I checked with the school and, just as I feared, I was out of the running for a contract.

The co-coordinator of the east San Jose district asked me if I would be willing to take a class for Severely Emotionally Disturbed children for one week. I was hesitant to take it for even one week, but found myself hanging on week after week, as the regular teacher was on leave because she herself had become emotionally disturbed.

The first week I found out why. Eight children ages 8 to 10 were each at different learning levels. Behavior was a major problem. There was a capable teacher's aide who had been with the class for many years.

My second day the aide was on duty in the play yard before school when a boy began strangling another child, until the victim was turning blue. My helper pulled him away, as he hit and kicked her, until she was bruised and bleeding. The child was sent to Juvenile Hall and the teacher's aide resigned.

During Spring break we made a trip to Omaha where Scott and Laurie had moved with their family. I told them about the problems I was having with my job.

"Why do you keep working at that job?" Scott asked me. "Is it for the money? If it is, maybe you should reconsider."

I didn't want to admit it, but that was the reason. I didn't want to miss out on another opportunity for a contract. I found out that with the wrong motive, nothing will succeed.

Like the regular teacher, I too became emotionally disturbed. Even though I tried hard to believe, repeating Philippians 4:13, *"I can do all things through Christ who strengthens me,"* I felt harassed day and night wherever I was.

I had been working with the class for four weeks. A visiting preacher came to our church on Easter Sunday. He shared how God had healed him from a terminal illness when he was at the point of death, encouraging us to have faith for miracles. Then he gave a word of knowledge.

"There is someone here this morning who is being harassed by a spirit of fear of failure," he announced. "You look back on your life and feel that you have always failed. It is getting so that you can't make a decision. If that describes you, please come up here, I believe Got wants to set you free."

At the moment I didn't feel I had failed at everything in my life, but God knew more about what was in my heart than I did. I knew I was being harassed. I was the first to go to the front of the little gathering. Others went up as well.

As I waited for my turn to receive prayer, I involuntarily let out a scream and fell forcefully to the floor. The next thing I knew the preacher was helping me to my feet. To my embarrassment, he turned me to face the group.

"This woman is not going to let Satan walk all over her any more!" he said.

Later someone told me I was smiling broadly, and didn't appear to be at all embarrassed. I felt totally relieved and free from the oppression. When I returned to my seat, two women came and told me what they felt God wanted to say to me.

"God showed me a picture of three precious stones, set in a ring," said one. "That is how you look to God. He loves you very much."

"And he has given you a new name" announced the other.

"Do I have to change my name?" I asked dubiously.

"It's up to you, but he told me your new name is Naomi."

I decided to keep the name a secret between myself and God unless he let me know differently.

I remembered the preacher had said I was afraid to make a decision. As soon as I could I notified the school that I would not be returning. They then hired a teacher who had the training and experience to handle the class.

In spite of all of my problems, I believe I was able to help some of the children. While I was with the class I visited the parents of two children, encouraging them that God would help them.

It was a year later, I got a delightful job teaching kindergarten in a Christian school, that I felt impressed to ask people to call me Naomi. I felt comfortable with the name God gave me. He had changed my life and given me a new start so why wouldn't he change my name?

It was a good time to do it because I was working with people who hadn't known me as Millie. Claude wanted to wait until we left the country before calling me by my new name.

I used to ask God to wake me up early in the morning so I would have time to pray and read the Bible before starting the day. He used a strange way of waking me up. I would hear Claude's voice calling me, "Millie!"

One morning I dreamed Claude's voice said, *"Naomi?"* in an incredulous tone of voice. I told him about the dream, and he laughed.

"It would mean so much to me, if you would call me the name the Lord gave me," I pleaded. He called me Naomi from then on.

The Uncomfortable Nest

The eagle is an example of how God helps us mature. When she builds her nest of sticks, the female pulls the soft feathers out of her breast to line it. After laying her eggs and incubating them, she feeds her eaglets until they have their flight feathers. She removes the soft feathers from the nest. It becomes uncomfortable for the fledglings on the sharp sticks, so they begin to leave the nest.

When we returned to our mother church, we felt like those fledgling eagles The name of the church was changed, from Gospel Temple, to Christian Community Church, a more acceptable term for today's population.

The leadership had enthusiastically led the people to give generously for our support in Brazil, but when it came to a boat ministry, the time was over, and we were preparing to be self supporting. However, we needed people behind us who would be our spiritual and prayer support.

Joanne Cardoza, a young friend of ours, told us about a church that grew out of the Jesus movement on the North coast of California. Some of the hippies who flowed into San Francisco in 1967 traveled up California State Highway 101 and settled in Mendocino and Humboldt Counties in the Redwood forested Coastal areas.

Jim Durkin, a pastor in Eureka, a small city on Humboldt Bay, was asked by some young converts to be their mentor. He took on the project, and started Lighthouse Ranch, where they lived communally on Table Bluff overlooking the Pacific Ocean. Out of this grew a church they called GO, acronym for Gospel Outreach. Jesus said, *"GO and preach the good news to all nations,"* and they did. Teams went out to core cities such as Chicago, the state of Alaska, and on into Germany, France, and Central America.

We began to get acquainted with GO by driving the 300 miles, visiting on holiday weekends. Pastor Jim and Dacie, his wife, made time for us, and understood our calling to missions.

The Lord put it in our hearts to invest in a reasonably priced house in King Salmon, a fisherman's village on a canal south of Eureka. We continued to rent it to the occupant, Nancy.

"I will have to move unless I find a job," she warned us. She had been unsuccessfully searching for a position as a elementary school teacher.

"Come to church with us Sunday," I suggested, "and ask God to give you a job."

She followed through, and a position opened in a school a mile from the house. Also it was her favorite grade level, third grade.

One day we were visiting on another boat with a young couple who lived at the same marina.

"We have a vision to go out on a missions trip on our boat. That's why we named her *Destiny*," Claude said.

The young wife spoke God's mind when she burst out, "Don't just talk about it and not do it!"

God spoke to us in many ways during the three years we commuted from the Marina to our jobs and to church. One place where we received direction was at a weekend gathering called "Festival of the Son," sponsored by GO. After hearing an impassioned young pastor preach about the world's hunger for God, and Jesus' commandment to go, we looked at each other and said, "We need to be about the Father's business NOW!"

We became driven to define a specific destination, thinking of going south down the coast of Mexico. On one of our trips to Eureka we met Dan and Linda York, who lived in Willow Creek in the Trinity Alps, east of Eureka. On weekends they stayed on

Gold Eagle, their 40-foot trimaran, berthed at Woodley Island near town.

Together we discussed our dreams. They were interested in sailing Gold Eagle and going to Central America with us, but lacked the finances.

"We need several minor miracles for that to happen," Dan said. He was a realtor, and would need to sell several properties. He asked us to pray they could sell enough real estate to pay for the outfitting and the loss of income so that they could go with us.

GO's South American churches had formed Verbo Ministries to supervise the missions they started in Central and South America. We read in the May 1991 issue of Verbo Ministries *Front Line Report:*

"In 1976 GO sent a team to Guatemala City to help rebuild after a severe earthquake left 250,000 homeless. In two years they built hundreds of houses for the homeless, school buildings, bridges, and helped local congregations build their meeting halls.

"While we extended ourselves to the needy, God began saving the upper middle class of Guatemalan society. A vibrant, growing church was born."

Bob and Myra Trolese, part of the team sent to Guatamala, were sent to Managua, Nicaragua, and founded a church there.

"Guatemala has had a lot of attention, I would be more interested in Nicaragua," said Claude. We decided to talk with Bob Trolese when he came to Eureka.

"We have a church on the east coast of Nicaragua, in Bluefields. I think you should go and give them a hand," he suggested. In 1988 Bluefields had been ravaged by a hurricane that camped over the city for 45 minutes, destroying most of the homes.

A 30 year civil war raged between the Sandanista Communist government and Contras, backed by the United States CIA. At that time Nicaragua was the third poorest country in the world.

"There is one problem," Claude told Pastor Trolese. "My brother is a high ranking deputy in the intelligence sector of the CIA."

"Well, yes, as a matter of fact, the biggest part of the Nicaraguan government's budget goes towards intelligence." began Bob.

"They will find out about that, but by watching you, they will see that you aren't in the same business as your brother."

Months later we received a letter from the Yorks. "We just got back from a class where we learned how to have faith to pray and see people healed. Now we feel we have something to offer in Nicaragua."

They flew to Bluefields to get acquainted with the church Bob had told us about. It was a rough trip by land, dangerous because of the contras. Upon their return they showed us a video and spoke enthusiastically about going there.

With all of this encouragement, we began to make plans to sail to Bluefields.

We spent a total of $10,000 outfitting the boat. We got a ham radio used by many ships at sea. At times you could get weather reports. The ham radio would reach almost anywhere in the world, but you had to learn Morse code and take a class in the technology to receive a license.

Claude asked me to sign up for a class, because he didn't think he had time to do it, outfit the boat, and make preparations for the trip. He asked me to get the license, which was a lot to ask. My verbal skills are high, but my science and math poor. He assured me that he would be praying for me, and God would help me pass. I finally passed, with God's help, on the second attempt.

Through the ham radio, we were able to stay in touch with our family at home by telephone patches like we did on the Jacaranda. We also were able to make contacts with people who knew where we were and where we were going. Safety was our watchword.

We had electronic devices such as a wind meter, depth sounder, radar, and a grounding plate for protection against lightning, two anchors and a storm sail. We also procured a desalinator, an El Toro dingy, an inflatable dingy and a life raft.

The two most useful pieces of equipment were the GPS and the autopilot. We purchased paper charts of the waters ahead. We feel these are better than today's electronic software.

Claude took a class in navigation. I went one night, and learned all I needed to know, in spite of sporadically nodding off to sleep following a hard day teaching my kindergarten class.

Having done all this, we felt we were ready to go.

CHAPTER SEVEN

We Weigh Anchor On "Our Destiny"

We had an "open boat" for all our friends and family the afternoon before we left. Our church, Pleasanton Community, previously had laid hands on us, praying with encouraging words and now many of them were touring the boat.

"Grandpa!" yelled five-year-old Alex, running into the cabin, "start up the engine and take us out for a spin!" When we just laughed he insisted all the more, "Mama said!"

Knowing his Mama, I shook my head smiling, "She was kidding, Alex!"

The next morning we motored out of our berth at Redwood City as our neighboring live-boarders, Larry and Dottie Turk, jumped up and down on the dock in excitement shouting, "Write if you find work," the cruisers' traditional goodbye. They soon would be setting out on a cruise and could hardly wait.

Arriving in San Francisco Bay, we stopped at Sausalito for more anchor chain, then headed to Angel Island. There we tied up to a mooring. I was in the galley below preparing dinner when Claude called me to come up into the cockpit.

"Look at those egrets!" he exclaimed. I looked, and saw six or eight egrets returning to a tree, with long necks sticking out of the foliage. They turned their heads this way and that as though they had been startled. Before I came up, Claude saw about 20 egrets flying up from of the island. He launched our El Toro, "Des-tiny," and started rowing ashore.

As he passed a boat moored nearby the skipper called out, "Did you hear about the earthquake?"

Claude said he hadn't.

"It just happened!" he replied. "It registered 7 points on the Richter scale. The upper deck of the Oakland Bay Bridge collapsed!"

On another boat there was a television. We stared in amazement as a reporter interviewed a confused woman in San Francisco's tenderloin district. Apartment buildings were ablaze with uncontrollable flames in the background. Lines of type ran across the bottom of the screen indicating the Bayshore freeway broke up and was closed. The epicenter was in the Santa Cruz Mountains.

Later when it was dark we could see explosions bursting into flames across the bay on the east shore, in Richmond where oil refineries were located.

The third game of the 1989 world series had just opened when the stadium shook and the Oakland Coliseum had to be evacuated. The initial jolt and evacuation were seen all over the world on live television.

It was very strange that we did not feel the impact that other boaters felt in the Pacific. One boater said he was knocked out of his shower. Another reported seeing the light poles swaying on the dock, and a skipper who was underway thought the engine threw a rod.

"Maybe we shouldn't leave!" I worried. "What if Grant's family needs help?"

"What could we do?" Claude said, "We sold our cars. We couldn't get through anyway because freeways are closed."

For seven years we had prayed and hoped, scraped and planned for this moment! Not even a major earthquake of this scale could dampen our excitement as we began the voyage.

At daylight we cast off, sailing toward the Golden Gate Bridge. We seemed to be the only boat on the bay.

"I read in the manual for the VHF radio that you can make phone calls," I told Claude. "I'm going to try to call Grant."

I picked up the microphone and switched on a channel. It was the first time I had used this handy communication tool.

"I have been ferrying people across the bay in my boat," a fisherman was saying.

Following the instructions in the manual, I reached the operator.

"Could you connect me with my son in San Jose?" I asked. "I want to see if his family is alright." We had no account with the company, but because of the emergency, he was happy to oblige.

"Groceries were knocked off shelves in the markets," Grant said, "but aside from a few things falling off shelves we are fine!" He added, "God totally spared San Jose!"

As we talked, I was reassured that our grandchildren were frightened, but unharmed. Grant's in-laws had come down from their house on the hillside, to spend the night with Grant and Debbie. Their home was closer to the epicenter and all the windows and glassware had broken, littering the floors with broken glass. But, thank God, that did not happen in Grant's house.

As we sailed under it, the Golden Gate Bridge was strangely silent. The mayor had called off all work for the day, and there was no traffic. With very few lights the city itself had an eerie feeling. The friends who were planning to take their boats out to see us off never showed up.

Claude Continues:

Never having been to sea by ourselves before, we were a little apprehensive. It was all up to us, "Sink or swim!" you might say. Yet we knew we could not sink, because God was with us. It was the beginning of the fulfillment of his plan for us.

"If God is for us, who can be against us? We can do all things through Christ, who strengthens us," was our conviction.

We would soon find out how true these Bible promises were. It seems that we must get into an impossible situation before we call on God with real faith and see him move miraculously. Why is it that we are so slow to ask and believe? Is it our pride, or is it because we live in a world where everything is at our fingertips? We don't think we need God, always relying on ourselves.

Claude and Naomi Kerr

The Bible says, "*You do not receive because you do not ask. Ask and you will receive, seek and you will find, knock, and it will be opened.*" (James 4:2, Luke 11:9)

If nothing else, this trip would be a good training school for teaching us these simple truths.

We sailed south along the coast for the first day and night. As we approached Monterey we saw our first miracle. It is common all along the California coast for afternoon fog to roll in, especially in the summer.

We were crossing Monterey Bay at about 3:00 pm when we began to see an approaching fog bank. We had visibility the rest of the way to the marina, because there was a circle of blue sky about a mile wide that followed us.

The next morning we met a couple who had been lost all night in the fog. They heard other ships, but did not know exactly where they were. All they knew to do was to dull their fears with a bottle of wine.

When we entered the marina we heard amplified instructions from the harbormaster.

"The sailboat coming in, take berth number 27." His voice grew exasperated, when we passed the berth and did not pull in there. It was already occupied by half a dozen big sea lions lounging on the dock.

Finding no other vacancies, we pulled in. The animals slipped into the water and swam towards a pier, barking indignantly as they went. We could hear a herd under the pier claiming its territory, barking back as they approached.

We went to bed, but were awakened at 3:00 am when the sea lions returned. I got up to chase them off. They pulled our power cord loose and I had to drag it into the cabin to fix it. The next morning we had their hair all over the cabin, a reminder of the early morning adventure with the power cord.

We were impatient to leave, but delayed for a week, as we waited for a fog free morning. It gave us an opportunity to visit with friends who lived in the area. When we left we headed for San Luis Obispo, where I used to live when I was in high school. It brought back pleasant memories of swimming and body surfing at Avila Beach.

We arrived at the pier after a rough night of sailing in strong wind. We learned a few things that night. I did not want to risk trying to find my way into the channel in the dark, so we waited offshore until it was light. It was a relief to enter into calm water behind a large breakwater, safe and secure.

Our next destination was Santa Barbara, where we were going to meet Dan and Linda York. They had left Eureka before we left San Francisco. It would be nice to have a "buddy boat." We wanted to arrive in Santa Barbara in late afternoon, or at least before dark, so we had to leave San Luis at about 10:00 pm and sail all night.

Although the auto pilot did the steering, we had to take turns standing watch just to look out for other boats during the night. The one on watch plotted our course on the navigational chart by getting longitude and latitude readings from the GPS, (global positioning satellite) instrument.

Naomi took the first watch at 7:00 pm, while I slept. I got up at 10:00 pm and kept watch until 1:00 am, then I took over until 4:00 am. The weather felt good. Point Conception is dreaded by sailors, but it was perfectly calm for us. We arrived in Santa Barbara at 2:30 pm, just as we had hoped. That was an average of 6 knots per hour.

Naomi's Childhood Memories

Santa Barbara was my birthplace. In 1933, when I was born, it was not the crowded vacation resort it is today. "Advanced technology" meant switching from stop signs on Main Street to electric stop signals with a stop sign that flipped up.

When the fast streamliner began to come through town, my father would drive the whole family down to the railroad track on Sunday nights just to watch it streak past as it went through town. Other Sunday evenings we got to go for a drive after dark, to window shop and "to see the wiggle waggles", Mama's name for neon lights.

Our berth at the yacht club was near the breakwater where our family used to go for evening walks. It is still in use, complete with a concrete promenade, old fashioned street lights, and concrete benches.

Claude and Naomi Kerr

My sister Dorothy had fond memories of our hometown as well, and she and her husband Bill drove up from Long Beach to visit with us. I remember Bill sitting in the stern next to the propane tank when I smelled a disgusting odor. He was not the guilty one, I found out, because propane tanks give off an odor when they are depleting.

During our stay in Santa Barbara we and the Yorks did some last minute work on our boats. One job necessitated going up the mast in the boson's chair, a seat that looks like an adult size infant swing. It was hauled up the mast with the aid of a manual winch.

"I should be the one to go up, since I weigh 115, and you weigh 180," I told Claude.

He was a little hesitant, but agreed. This was not easy for me, because of the vertigo that I always felt from heights, and the mast was 53 feet high. Once I was on top, I threaded a line through a block. Later he had me pull up some tools fastened to a line, and there was a delay as he tried to work out what I should do next. Then he finally lowered me down. He had to do it himself, he explained, because he had to see the situation before he could fix it.

I volunteered to go up the mast.

In the meantime, on the York's boat, Dan's son Tom, 20, kept Dan and Linda informed on how long I had been up the mast.

110

"She's been up there 15 minutes."

"Twenty minutes, and she's still up there!"

"Forty minutes, can you believe it?"

"He's letting her down after forty five minutes!"

Linda joked with Claude, "Tell the truth, you were trying to get even with her for something!"

I was not eager to go through that again, and am glad that I never had to do it again for the rest of my time at sea.

Dan York had served in the Navy Seals, and was an expert scuba diver. Many times this skill came in handy. On their way down the coast they anchored for the night in a cove 50 miles north of Santa Barbara near Point Conception.

Dan's son Tom was the first one to notice water coming into the cabin through the rudder pipe. They called the Coast Guard and a rescue boat came out and towed them to Santa Barbara.

Rather than make a new rudder, Dan thought he would try to dive to recover the one that fell off at the cove. so he and Linda drove back up the coast to try and find it.

"On the way I was thinking, 'What are the chances that I can find that rudder in just one day?'" recalled Dan. "So I asked the Lord to help me. I left Linda on the shore and tried to go where we might have been anchored. On my very first dive I went right to it! I thank God for that!"

The Yorks left for Newport Beach where they wanted to complete their preparations near Linda's family. We wanted to stay in Santa Barbara, and our only disappointment was that we never got out to the Channel Islands, where we had wanted to go on our honeymoon.

We continued hopping from marina to marina until we got to Newport Beach where Dan and Linda on Gold Eagle were already berthed. There the yacht club would not allow us to take a berth at their marina, because they would not honor our membership in the Humboldt Bay Yacht Club. We were forced to anchor in the bay. I phoned my niece, Kathy Schwab, who lived with her family in Orange County.

"Come on down here and see our boat," I said. She arrived on the appointed day, bringing her daughter, Melissa, with her. I didn't think to tell her that we were anchored out, and they would have to ride out to Destiny in the dingy.

"When we saw that we would have to ride with you in that little tiny boat to your boat way out in that choppy water," she told us later, "we were petrified with fear!"

Hiding their emotions, they climbed into the dingy with me. I got them there safely, although it was the first time I had driven Des-Tiny with the outboard rather than using oars.

Before they left, Kathy handed me an envelope. "John and I wanted to give you something for your mission," she said. I thanked her and put it in my pocket.

Soon a vacancy occurred at a public dock where we tied up Claude began to work on the engine, which had conked out once or twice. He was not able to stop it from overheating, so he hired an engine mechanic to work on it.

After the mechanic left, Claude was tightening something when the screwdriver he was using dropped inside the engine. This caused him a great deal of frustration. I wanted to help him somehow. At that moment I remembered the envelope in my pocket.

"Lets see what Kathy and John gave us," I said, as I opened the envelope.

I couldn't believe what I saw. It was full of $20 bills.

"You will not believe this, $1,000!" I exclaimed. "Now you can afford to get the mechanic back…. He will get the screwdriver out."

Of course Claude was still disgusted with himself for dropping it in there, but he did call the mechanic. We had to make sure we would have a functioning engine before we left the country.

Claude Continues the Story

We continued our marina hopping until we arrived at San Diego. This was our last chance to get any equipment or spare parts we needed before leaving the good old USA. All we lacked before leaving was a large assortment of stainless bolts and screws. In San Diego we went to a fishing shop and asked what lures to use for trolling in Mexico and Central America. We bought two lures, one yellow and bright green, the other green and blue.

Shipping regulations call for all vessels traveling in foreign waters to fly the flag of the country whose waters they are traversing as well as the flag of one's home country. At the nautical flag shop a friendly lady proprietor helped us choose an American flag. When we saw how the price would add up for the flags of all the countries we would be passing, we were not happy.

"If you have a sewing machine you can make your own," the shop owner suggested. "Then you can make flags as you need them."

"I have a baby Singer, and I think I could do that," said Naomi.

She supplied us with a chart of most flags of the world and a bag full of colored remnants, all gratis!

"It is refreshing to do business with decent people like you," she said with a smile. "Nowadays I get so many customers who are sailing south to trade in drugs!"

Once, later in our trip, we lost our American flag in a gale. We sure didn't want to attempt to make an American Flag, but discovered that cruisers help each other with needed items. At the next port we asked if anyone had an extra American flag. A skipper had one and gave it to us. We found out they needed a flag for their next destination, and Naomi made one in exchange.

We were told we had to stop in Ensenada, only 70 nautical miles away, because it was Mexico's port of entry. We checked in and paid all the fees, including an expensive fishing license required for all boats. No one can resist the great fishing in Mexican waters! This procedure took all day.

Dan and Linda made friends with a customs official, who spoke excellent English. But Naomi decided to try out her Spanish. She took several classes in Spanish before leaving the States. The summer before she enrolled in a crash course that covered college Spanish 1, 2, and 3. She rattled off something in Spanish.

He stared at her with a perplexed look, "That's Portuguese!" he exclaimed.

Linda laughed in delight, but Naomi was embarrassed.

"I worked with some Brazilians on a ship," said the official, "and I learned some of the words."

It is very difficult to keep the two languages separated, as they share much of the same vocabulary.

We were happy to leave Ensenada to begin the real trip into the unknown. We had a good shakedown cruise to Ensenada, and were eager to take off into the "wild blue yonder." We had traveled 600 miles from San Francisco, and it took approximately two months because of long delays in Santa Barbara and Newport Beach.

Due to our GPS we felt confident. They first came into use during my last year working for the county. At the time we left one could pick up satellites only nine hours a day and were accurate within 30 feet. Today they are available 24 hours a day and accurate within three feet.

We had a nice wind and were sailing along at 5 knots. It was good we could sail, because in spite of the mechanic's work our engine still overheated and stopped periodically.

Wherever we could anchor we stopped for the night to avoid having to sail through the night. We stopped in San Quintin Bay, on the Pacific Coast of Baja California, and left at 8:00 am.

Naomi's Story

This began a slow day's sail. At 7:00 pm we began a spooky night passage. We on *Destiny* and the Yorks on *Gold Eagle* decided to pass between Isla Cedros and the Baja California shoreline. It turned out to be a bad decision. To begin with there was a heavy bed of kelp. Then Dan radioed us.

"Hey, pray for us! Our water pump quit!"

Without a water pump, the engine cannot be cooled.

"We'll head over towards you to help," Claude answered. It was not long, after changing our course, that our propeller caught in the kelp and stalled our engine. We prayed and it started up again.

After sunset darkness set in, with no stars or moon visible. Only our contact with the Gold Eagle dispelled the eerie silence. At 12:25 am our engine quit again.

"Sorry buddy," Claude radioed Dan, explaining our problem. "I'm afraid you're on your own now!"

"That's OK," Dan replied. "I filled the bilge with water and rigged up the bilge pump to cool the engine.

We both came into *Bahia Tortugas*, (Turtle Bay) at noon. We arrived at the anchorage, dropped anchor, and the engine died!

We thanked the Lord it did not stop until we arrived. Meanwhile the Gold Eagle had anchored near land at the bay entrance to do some fishing. Then it started pouring, a torrential rain so heavy you could not see across the channel. That gave us a chance to fill up our water tanks. Once the deck was washed, we removed the filler caps to the tanks on port and starboard decks, and they filled up in 20 minutes.

Then the Yorks arrived, and we launched Des-Tiny to go over to Gold Eagle to compare sea stories.

"We caught a beautiful albacore on our troll line," Dan said, "but when we brought it in only the head was left on the hook. A shark ate the rest. Then the fishing line was caught on the prop so the engine quit. 'Oh God help me,' I thought, 'I'm going to have to dive down and clear the prop even if there is a shark down there!' Thank God, he protected me!"

Later in our trip, we met a cruising couple who were experienced at sailing the Isla Cedros passage we had just completed.

"We never go between the island and the shore. It is dangerous and unpredictable in those waters."

Claude Continues

Dan's water pump went out due to a bad bearing.

"Its doubtful we can find a Mercedes inboard bearing here in Turtle Bay," Dan said.

"Yeah, this is an isolated place," I agreed.

We went ashore and found some mechanics working in a large desalinator plant. Molecules of salt water are smaller than bacteria, and the process produces pure drinking water for the town. With our poor Spanish we tried to communicate our problem, and showed them the bad bearing.

They started pounding it to get it loose, laughing and talking while they worked, probably laughing at us two "gringos." In a short time they had the bearing off, giving it to a young man who went away with it. He shortly came back with a brand new bearing in a box wrapped in paper. It fit, praise the Lord! Who would have thought you could find that particular part in a place like Turtle Bay?

"*Cuanto Cuesta?*" we asked.

"*Treinta dollars,*" they answered.

Thirty dollars! We thought that was the best bargain in the world.

There were about four other American couples anchored nearby. On our last night all ten of us decided to eat at one of the little stands where the local residents sold tacos made with freshly barbecued meat.

After walking up and down the street checking out all the stands, all ten of us made the mistake of converging on one stand all at once. That was our only food for dinner, so Claude and I kept ordering one more. That was a mistake as well, because they didn't cook it long enough.

We weighed anchor soon after our meal, and we hadn't gone far when we both experienced symptoms of food poisoning. Naomi occasionally was seasick, but I got my sea legs before I could walk. My first ocean crossing was taken at the age of two weeks when my parents returned from the Philippines where I was born. My father had a job surveying for a railroad near Manila.

My Dad used to say, "Claude and I were the only ones who went to the dining room. All the other passengers were seasick."

That was the only time I lost it, and I attribute it to the food. It was one of the times it was good to have our buddy boat within sight. Dan radioed us.

"You look like you are off course," he said. "What's wrong?"

Checking the compass we saw he was right and made an adjustment.

"We're both sick," we explained. "Thanks for watching out for us!"

Two days later we had recovered and we anchored at *Bahia Santa Maria*. It was timely to be at St. Mary's Island for it was Christmas eve. A *panga* (an open boat with an outboard motor) pulled up alongside, and A local fisherman with his son looked up at us. As the young teen-age boy looked on with an expectant smile, his father asked us in Spanish if we wanted to trade something for four lobster tails.

All we had for Christmas dinner was a little can of turkey, and we were very glad to make a deal. They asked for American magazines.

"We have no magazines," we said, "Is there anything else you want?" They understood our Spanish, and he asked if we had any T shirts or hats. Dashing into the cabin, we picked out all the T Shirts with writing or pictures on them, and found a couple of sun visors. Those pleased them very much, and they gave us the lobster in exchange. Those used shirts and visors were probably the boy's Christmas present.

The lobster provided a delicious Christmas dinner for ourselves and Dan and Linda. Tom had gone home by then. We were so excited about following Jesus on this adventure that we didn't feel any sorrow for not being with family for Christmas, plus we were with some of God's big family.

Jesus said, *"Those who listen to me and do my will are my mother and brothers."*

Our first major goal was to reach Cabo San Lucas, 1,677 miles from San Francisco. We were there in two more days.

Cabo was a sports fisherman's paradise. From our anchorage we watched one fisherman after another pose with a marlin higher than himself strung from a crossbar for a picture. One of the cruisers caught one and invited all the rest of us for a marlin barbecue.

Sunday was also New Year's Eve, and I got on the VHF and asked if anyone knew of a nearby church. A cruising woman who become a permanent resident with a home ashore told us of a Nazarene church that had been founded by an American missionary couple. She assured us we would feel at home there.

We went for the Sunday morning service. The small congregation filled the building to capacity. Their singing was lively and enthusiastic. We recognized most of the songs from our churches at home. The founders, Johnnie and Marie Lynch, were there, white haired and in their late 70s.

We went back for the evening service. Since it was New Year's Eve, at the conclusion of the service everyone in the building, both young and old, enthusiastically hugged everyone there, as they wished each other *"bueno ano."*

The pastor invited us to his home, where we were able to converse with a number of folks from the church. They appeared to be the leaders. A few teen aged girls sat in front of a small Christmas tree and exchanged inexpensive gifts.

It was amazing how much the Lynchs were able to do without having ever learned to speak the language. The pastor, however, and several others could speak English, and everyone gathered around a piano and sang Christmas carols in English. They really honored their founders in every way.

Promptly at midnight all the wives came out of the kitchen where they had been preparing a dinner, and kissed their husbands. The meal began with a savory soup of shellfish, served with sourdough French bread. The rest of the dinner was like an American Thanksgiving or Christmas dinner, with a stuffed roast turkey and all the traditional side dishes.

A few days later we decided we should leave for Mazatlan, since the Yorks were already there waiting for us. This passage was crossing the Sea of Cortez from Baja to the mainland of Mexico. We left early in the evening.

Naomi's Account:

When I went below for my turn to sleep, the seas were very "lumpy," with ten foot swells quite close together. It felt like the boat would drop and hit the water with a bang every time we descended. The sea was deafening, a ceaseless roar, like a noisy freight train.

Holding on tightly to the rails and grab bars was necessary whenever I stood up. We had a board to fit into the side of the berth, preventing us from rolling out. I had no trouble dropping off to sleep, thanks to my constant use of Dramamine.

My lack of fear was amazing. When I was freed from the spirit of fear of failure, I was also set free from other fears. My faith in God's protection was strengthened with every dangerous situation we had faced ever since we left. Reading the Bible day by day, I made note of every mention of God's control over seas and storms. Believing Jesus lived in me gave me faith. I firmly believed I could exercise the same authority that Jesus had when He was on earth!

God Got Us Through

As we left for Mazatlan the weather was perfect for sailing. Ten to fifteen knot winds carried us along at maximum hull speed of 7 knots. We radioed the boats in Cabo to report the balmy conditions. However, that didn't last long! It was 2:00 am while Naomi was sleeping down below when the swells reached 10 foot.

I began to pray earnestly. Considering the weather, we were not on the best course. The wind was coming off our beam at right angles to our intended course. Consequently we rolled with the

OUR DESTINY

arrival of each wave. It was beginning to get a little light at 5:00 am when Naomi came up for her watch. I asked her to go below and look at the wind speed indicator.

"Its gusting up to 50 knots!" she exclaimed. She had never seen the pointer that far around the dial before.

"I don't know what to do," I admitted. "I don't want to go bare poles, with no sail, because this wind could drive us far out to sea. I've already got the sail reefed as far as it will go. Maybe I should take the sail down and put up the storm sail. The sail maker said it can take up to 70 knots."

"We need to pray!" declared my spiritual wife.

I am very practical minded, and I snapped back, "What do you think I've been doing for the last three hours? I've been doing nothing *but* praying!"

"Yes," she insisted, "but Jesus said when we *agree together* He would answer!"

My mind flashed back to something she told me when we were making our plans for this trip.

"I will go to sea with you on one condition!" she said.

I snapped to attention. "What is your condition?"

"That you pray with me!" She was terribly worried when our last captain had refused to join our prayer meeting on the deck. The wind and the engine had stopped and we were uncertain where we were in relation to Majuro.

"OK," I said meekly. "Lets pray together."

The main part of our short prayer was like Jesus spoke during a storm on the Sea of Galilee.

"Don't you care if we drown?" said the disciples, as they shook the sleeping Jesus.

"*Where is your faith?*" he responded. Then he stood up and commanded the wind and waves to stop, and they did. The disciples marveled, "*even the wind and waves obey his commands.*"

Naomi and I held onto the guard rail with one hand and each other with the other as we commanded the wind to stop. Then I lowered the sail and hoisted the storm sail, and went below to bed. Fifteen minutes later I heard a new sound and poked my head out of the cockpit.

"Now what? Oh! The wind had stopped! I lashed down the boom, which was the reason for the crashing sound I had heard.

I fired up the engine, which worked. Another pleasant surprise, or perhaps another miracle. Contented, I went to sleep.

When I got up about an hour later a light wind had picked up, and we were able to sail with a full main. No one would deny that God stopped the wind. The same Jesus whose authority stopped the wind on the lake of Galilee lives inside of us and will take action when we have faith. It seems that when we are in desperate situations we have more faith.

We continued towards Mazatlan. It was about 7:00 am, when I noticed a huge Princess line cruise ship ahead. I couldn't figure out what his course was, and I wanted to steer clear of him, so I radioed him.

"This is Destiny calling to the cruise ship. What is your course and your destination?" I asked. The captain answered with a clipped but friendly British accent.

"Our destination is Mazatlan. What is your speed, Destiny?"

"Five and a half knots."

He laughed, saying, "Well, you are the overtaking vessel, we are only doing 4 knots."

The rules of the sea are such that the overtaking vessel does not have the right-of-way, regardless of its size. I still couldn't tell which direction he was headed.

"We are going around in circles so that we will arrive at our port at 8:00 am so that the passengers can watch as we come in," the captain explained.

"Can you pick us up on your radar?" was my next question. He said he could, and that was comforting to know.

As the night went on we were entertained by a conversation between that captain, who said he was new on his ship, and the captain of another ship about the disposal of the garbage. "No one wants to take responsibility for the gah-badge!" was his problem.

When we arrived at Mazatlan at 6:30 am the engine had quit again. We anchored in a yacht basin crowded with too many boats. It was the first time I had anchored only by wind power. It was easier with the motor, but we found it was possible under sail too.

The Gold Eagle had found a better anchorage at Isla Piedra (Rock Island) very near Mazatlan. We joined them there. There was one other sailboat anchored nearby, and we went over to get acquainted. We found out the couple had made the passage from Cabo the same night as we did.

"It was a horrendous trip!" exclaimed the woman. They were using their genoa, a large forward sail, and the wind tore it to ribbons, then a huge wave broke over our boat and soaked everything in their cabin.

"We prayed,..." I began.

"Well we didn't!" snapped the woman.

We heard later that they were going to hire someone to return their boat to San Diego because they didn't want to sail again. Apparently they didn't carry through with it, because we met them again in Acapulco at a yacht club swimming pool. It was interesting how God arranged our meeting. I am sure that she remembered our previous conversation. As we were talking a man walked by who had just come across the Bay of Tehuanapec, a very rugged passage.

"How was your passage?" my friend asked.

"I'll tell you what, he responded, I'm not a religious man, but I prayed!"

Isla Piedra was an idyllic setting. On the beach was a shelter with a palm leaf thatched roof where a rotund Mexican Mama cooked wonderful tacos and burritos with homemade tortillas she patted out with her hands.

She had a 12 year old son who was a helper, and a good one. On Sunday we asked him to guide us to a church. We had decided to give our usual offering to local churches while on the trip, and that was one reason for our church hunting. We tried to explain the kind of church we were looking for. He seemed to understand, but took us to the home of some Jehovah's Witnesses.

We were speaking in Spanish, but finally told him, "A church where they say, 'Praise the Lord,' and Halleluiah". We demonstrated, lifting our hands in praise.

"A Halleluiah church?" he exclaimed, and took us up a steep path to the home of a family who attended *"La Iglesia Apostolica de Jesus Jesucristo,"* (Apostolic Church of Jesus Christ). Their church needed money for a building, so our offering was timely, and appreciated.

I had comic booklets about Jesus that my niece, Kathy, had sent us, and read through one of them with our young guide. He was very attentive. He also was grateful for a muumuu that I gave his mother.

The Island Where the Birds Lived

Our next destination was Isla Isabela, a little south and about 20 miles offshore. It is a small volcanic island. The little bay where we anchored was very rocky, but the water was clear, and you could see the bottom, so when we saw a patch of sand we dropped our anchor. The Gold Eagle anchored nearby.

There were no human inhabitants there, only birds. Thousands of seabirds nested there. The lower levels were covered with low bushes that were perfect for frigates. Boobies nested in the higher areas on the bare ground.

Frigates are large black birds that cannot take off from the ground or water. They nested on the bushes where they can take off to fly. The male's defense is a red pouch that hangs loosely from the front of their necks. They sit on the nests, guarding their eggs or chicks. To warn predators they blow up the pouch into a balloon and make a sound with their beaks hitting the balloon like a drum, "rat tat tat tat."

Frigate

Frigates are also known as man-of-war birds due to their habit of robbing other birds of food. The boobies, on the other hand, are excellent divers. They both survived and flourished on the same island, because the boobie dives and catches the fish, and the frigate follows after it and pesters it until it drops the fish, then swoops down to catch it in midair. Apparently the boobies catch enough for both.

The boobies were so nicknamed by British sailors. The official name is gannet. We often walked by them as they nested and they would stare at us, making no effort to get away.

Boobie and Chick

I aimed my camera at a mother who was sitting on a chick and waited until it peeked out from under her before shooting my picture.

Several boats left the island at the same time and sailed towards the mainland together. As we sailed we caught lots of yellow fin tuna with our troll lines, using the bright lure we bought in San Diego. A couple from Victoria, British Columbia, gave us a recipe for tuna jerky. After marinating it in a sauce, Naomi hung it over the life lines that lined the decks and, to our surprise, it dried in just one day.

Naomi's Story

One evening, after going ashore, we stopped at the Yorks boat on our way home.

"Did you leave your engine on to charge your generator?" Dan asked us. "We heard it running while you were gone.

Startled, we answered, no, we hadn't turned it on, and hurried back to find the engine was running, and we didn't know when or how it started.

"Do we have a ghost pilot?" I joked.

That night we were awakened at 3:00 am by the engine starting up. Claude bounded out of the berth, and went out to the cockpit, but no one was there. He turned the engine off and came back to bed.

Even though I do not believe in ghosts, it gave me a strange feeling. I prayed that God would show us what the trouble was. He told me two words, "moisture" and "solenoid." I did not know what a solenoid was. I knew what moisture was. I told Claude, but it didn't mean anything to him, either.

We had met a couple in Mazatlan from Victoria, BC, Mel and Diane Bacon. Mel was a mechanic. They were anchored nearby, so we went over and asked if he would check it out. He did, and explained it to us. It had to do with salt and moisture, as well as the solenoid.

He cleaned out the moisture and salt, and it never happened again.

We continued down the coast to Puerto Vallarta. The Yorks anchored near town free of charge, but we went a little further to Nuevo Vallarta, one of the three marinas we found in Mexico.

The others were in Acapulco and Isla Mercedes on the Yukatan Peninsula on the East Coast.

When we were still at home in San Jose we met the Pastor of a Spanish speaking church. We visited his church, and when he found we were going to Mexico he urged us to visit a church in Buserias, a city north of Puerto Valletta. Eager to reach out to them, we boarded a bus to Buserias

Again we had to ask directions to a church that was nameless to us.

"Where is the *Aleluia* church?" we asked at a grocery store. They directed us to a nearby church. Like many other churches in Mexico, they believed women must cover their heads. Since I didn't have a head covering, the pastor's wife gave me a large scarf which covered all my hair. The pastor had two houses and a car. He picked us up for the Sunday morning service.

A Canadian couple who lived in a condo in Puerto Vallarta also attended. They wanted to buy benches for the new building the church had just completed. The pastor asked me to interpret for him while he spoke to them.

No one was in the room except his wife, the Canadians, Claude and I. What he wanted to tell them was that he preferred they would give him cash rather than buy the benches, because, he said, he could get them cheaper by going into the mountains to buy wood.

The strange thing about this transaction was the pastor's wife wept profusely throughout the conversation. Her husband never asked her what was wrong. I could only suspect that he had ulterior motives.

Later we discovered another church that greatly appealed to us. It was a much larger group, of perhaps several hundred, meeting in a large shelter with a concrete floor. All the people seemed to be newly converted. Unlike the other church, it had no legalistic rules. There we sensed God's presence.

One Sunday an American missionary who spoke good Spanish preached He compared sin with leprosy, using many scriptures to illustrate leprosy. As with sin, leprosy was a debilitating disease leading to death. When he finished most of the people came to the front to be receive prayer.

Claude and I were invited to pray with them. I was surprised that, as soon as I touched them the power of God caused them to fall backwards to the concrete floor where they remained, peacefully resting in His presence. No one was hurt because unseen angels were easing them down.

Pastor Saul told us he was an architect before experiencing the power of God through the ministry of American missionaries. From the beginning the newly formed church began experiencing supernatural healings and conversions.

"One morning while I was sitting in church," he continued, God told me, 'You will even raise the dead!' After church I went to a hotel to pray for an American man who came to Mexico to die. He was suffering from cirrhosis of the liver.

"When I prayed for him, he was healed immediately. His whole family was flying down from the States dressed in black for his funeral. When they arrived he was swimming at the beach.

It was difficult to find the church because it had no name.

"In the Bible churches were named after their location," the pastor explained. "This one is the Church of Buserias," and our other churches around the area are named after the towns where they are located."

Naomi Teaches in Spanish

I told the pastor's wife that I felt God wanted me to speak to the women about prayer. It was not until after she accepted my offer that I discovered there would be no interpreter. Back in the boat, I began writing notes, using the English/Spanish dictionary and a Spanish Bible.

I felt that God wanted praying women to take the night watches in their homes to stand between the devil and God, praying for their families.

Linda York knew how hard it was for me to be understood in Ensenada, and I asked her to go with me to the women's meeting and to pray for me. They not only understood my message, but when I offered to pray for those who would be willing to be intercessors all of them gladly volunteered. Again, when I touched them there was evidence God also touched them. The pastor's wife fell down.

Magdalena, from Costa Rica, and her American boyfriend went to church with us.

She then asked me to speak to some women who were meeting on a weekday evening in an outlying town. I accepted her invitation and spoke on how a woman can win her husband to Christ without words if she relies on God and on her own Godly life.

Saul's wife was in tears as I talked about the need for us Christian women to respect our husbands, even when they don't do what they should. I have found this far more effective than preaching to him. (1 Peter 3:1)

It was a good thing we were delayed six weeks while Dan and Linda waited for repairs on their auto pilot, because God had a lot for us there. We met a couple on a boat named Tern. Carlos was American and his girlfriend, Magdalena, was Costa Rican. She had joined him as "crew" in Costa Rica.

They were traveling north, and had just traversed the gulf of Tehuantepec, one of the windiest passages in Mexico. He asked her father, a Costa Rican fisherman, how to make the passage.

"The way he told me, cutting straight across, might be fine for a big fishing boat," Carlos told us, "but it sure didn't work for me! When we got out in the middle of the bay I was nailed!"

Magdalena, who spoke perfect English, told me the rest of the story. The seas were so rough that when she was below in the cabin, her head kept hitting the ceiling.

"I went up on deck to see how Carlos was doing, and he was crying. I said, 'Carlos, pray! God can help you!' I prayed to Jesus, but he prayed to his dead grandmother! Anyway, God answered and we got here safely."

We invited them to church with us, and they came.

Later an evangelist had arrived from the States, and the churches all met together in a large hotel ballroom. None of the churches were big enough for the crowd.

Dan and Linda were there. Linda was very interested in a couple who went up on the stage revealing how God allowed them to have a child. This after many years of infertility.

After the prayer time Linda said, "God told me I would have a baby." I joined her in believing God can and will answer prayer.

While praying and dreaming of having their own child, they filled the void with a new pet. Linda and I were shopping at a local outdoor market in Zihuatanejo when we saw a box of, recently hatched birds, strange looking little creatures whose feathers had not yet grown. It turned out they were baby parrots. Linda bought one. We couldn't understand what the lady said they eat. She brought over a dish of a soupy gruel. There were also ants in the dish.

"They eat ants?" exclaimed Linda. I interpreted for her, and the merchant hastily explained it was thin corn meal mush. They fed their new baby with an eye dropper. He grew into a perky conure named Skipper.

It was very difficult for Linda to continue the voyage, for when far out of sight of land she became anxious.

"She cries, and then I lose my own confidence as a sailor," Dan said. They decided to send for Dan's son, Tom, to return to crew in her place, but Linda knew a son cannot replace a wife. She courageously stayed on for the most frightening part of the trip, crossing the gulf of Tehuantepec.

Claude and Naomi Kerr

Dan feeds Skipper with an eyedropper.

"I knew they wouldn't eat right if I didn't go and cook for them," she explained.

Claude decided to visit an American embassy along the way to be informed on the war in Nicaragua. We went there and got printouts of warnings. Simply stated, it was not advisable for Americans to go there. At the same time we heard that the United States had invaded Panama and arrested President Noriega. He was charged with shipping illegal drugs into our country. News reports told of casualties from street fighting during what was dubbed "Operation Just Cause."

Idyllic Spots In Mexico

We continued south, anchoring at some idyllic little bays. People were usually friendly and glad to see you, whereas in the larger tourist centers like Puerto Vallarta and Acapulco their hospitality always had a price tag. It doesn't help that some Americans give us a bad name by the way they behave.

A place that I would love to return to was Puerto Escondido, a beautiful, fair sized bay. A young American lady relaxing on the beach said she rented a hotel room for $156 a month. However, if you want to go there, remember that was back in 1990.

Navigating A Rugged Crossing

We joined with Gold Eagle before crossing the Gulf of Tehuantepec, spending the night anchored off a beach. It was not a good anchorage, but we wanted to wait there for some other sailboats we had contacted on the radio. It would be better to go as a group in case problems should arise. The others arrived in the morning.

There were eight boats in our caravan. I knew that some of us in the group were Christian believers, like Bob and Norma Leach on Hale Lana from Anchorage, Alaska, and Bill and Diana Katz, of Morning Star, Murray and Hazel Switzer on HMS Destiny, and, of course the Yorks.

I reasoned that, because of the stressful voyage we were embarking upon, others might be interested in praying for our trip as well. I got on the radio and made a suggestion:

"If anyone would like to pray for our safe passage, switch to channel five." Once I had switched myself, I conducted a roll call, then led in a prayer. It was gratifying that all those I just mentioned were listening, and I suspect the other two were there but hesitant to answer the roll call.

Diana Katz, fluent in Spanish and the last boat in line, lived in Mexico for several years and was fluent in Spanish. She had also picked up the polite expressions that show respect. She radioed the Mexican Coast Guard for weather information, and there were no reports of foul weather.

A cruiser familiar with the gulf passage had advised Claude early in our trip to, "Stick close enough to shore so you could hear the dogs bark." This was quite different from the advice of Magdalena's father, who had told Carlos to take the shortest route. Everyone who was with us seemed to know that.

After much apprehension, I was surprised at my own lack of fear. The sun was shining brightly, and there were rolling swells that we seemed to mount and ride like a surfer. The seas were moving in the same direction as we were, without breaking and without white caps. To me it was exhilarating. Standing at the wheel, I was reminded of the time I learned to sail the El Toro on Tamales Bay.

Linda York radioed us with a timorous voice, "How are the seas over there?" she asked.

"Just great! I think it's exhilarating!" I answered.

"Well I don't!" she replied.

"Remember, we prayed. God is with us," I reassured her.

All was not rosy for Mizpah, a boat up ahead of us, however.

"We have a leak!" the skipper announced.

"We are right behind you," responded Bob Leach on Hale Lana. "Let us know if you need us!" When we were in Nuevo Vallarta the Leachs had held a worship service on their boat. They surely were good Samaritans.

A half hour later Diana called from Morning Star, "Do you want me to call the Coast Guard?" she asked.

"No, no, it looks like the bilge pump is keeping up with it. I think it will be alright."

We Reach Our Safe Haven

We sailed all night. At 5:00 am we experienced squalls and thunder and lightning, with 60 miles left to reach our last port in Mexico, Puerto Madeiro. We did not arrive until 7:00 pm. There was heavy rain falling and it was dark.

Claude was on the radio with Hale Lana, "I can't see, and I'm not going in. We'll just sail around outside the harbor until morning," he said.

"I can see, said Bob. Follow me!" His eyesight was not very good, however, and he turned aside while I passed him.

"I can barely see two white lights that look like range markers," I said.

Dan York was guiding me on the radio, since he was already anchored and could see us coming. I told Bob to follow me. When I saw a red light Dan said to turn in, and I did. Bob didn't see whether I turned or not, so they went straight.

His wife groaned, "We went aground!" They had to wait there until the tide turned. In the meantime, we couldn't see where we were.

"Where do we go?" I was asking.

The comforting voice of an old, experienced cruiser came through, "You're right where you belong now. Drop your hook, take a shower... relax."

So we did. In the morning we looked out and saw we had come down a very narrow channel.

A Mexican man came up to Destiny in an open outboard.

"I will take you to church," he said. "I'll pick you up Sunday morning at 9:00 o'clock."

We were amazed that he said that, and we were ready and waiting Sunday morning. He took us ashore, and we got into his van.

He stopped and picked up other people who were waiting, then stopped and said, "Here is the church," then waited for us to get out.

"Aren't you coming?" I asked him.

"No," he said. "I'm not going."

It was then that I realized he had a route and he only provided transportation. I do not know how he found out that we wanted to go to church.

Like the one in Cabo San Lucas, the church was founded by an American missionary. He had married a Mexican woman. They lived in a big house, where they once ran an orphanage. He and his wife took us in. In the morning I saw a smiling woman come in the gate grasping a freshly killed chicken by the legs. I found out later she came to have a tooth extracted. She was happy that the missionary could take away her pain. The chicken was his payment.

"The first time I came to Mexico, I found out that the biggest source of pain was toothaches," our host explained. "I went home and took a course in dentistry."

He also founded three churches. To us he was an example of how a true apostle works. The national people were the ones who ran the churches. They did not need him any more.

"The first church was Baptist and the second one Nazarene," he said.

Claude asked what the third one would be. His response may have been influenced by talking with Claude:

"I don't know. Maybe it will be independent."

During the few days in Puerto Madeiro we had a taste of the local flavor. The little church we had attended had a memorial service in the home of an 18-year-old boy who had come to church and was saved. Tragically, later he went out in a boat when he was drunk, drowning in an accident.

At this sad occasion everyone had a song to offer. Two men would sing a hymn, then two little girls. This went on for some time. One of the men read from the Bible and spoke a few encouraging words about the continuance of life for the young man.

The boy's mother, who appeared to be quite elderly, was pleased to have the support. She had prepared an altar with lots of flowers and a picture of Mary above it. After the service she and her daughters served everyone a cup of rich Mexican chocolate and a homemade tamale.

One night shortly after our arrival we were sitting on the deck and saw a large boat blazing with lights and sound. The cruisers were venting their stress from the passage through Tehuantepec with alcohol and loud celebration.

From Puerto Madeiro it was only 15 miles to Guatamala, just over the border of Mexico. We had a great feeling of accomplishment. After sailing 2,726 nautical miles, we were full of God's peace and joy. It was a relief to me to have passed the long Mexican coastline.

We didn't stop in Guatamala, because the government was unstable at the time, and we didn't know of any reason why we should. Gospel Outreach had sent out a team to help with the earthquake many years before, resulting in a well developed church. We wanted to go to places that aren't easily accessible by major airlines and where the most needy and poorest people live. It is best if there aren't too many preachers already there.

It took 225 nautical miles and three days to pass Guatamala and El Salvador. Destiny and Gold Eagle were within sight of each other one night when we experienced some company. A military helicopter flew overhead, turning spotlights on us. In the morning a small boat crowded with soldiers arrived.

While I (Claude) was still asleep, Naomi talked with them on the radio. They asked if we were planning to stop in El Salvador. The government was concerned about weapons being smuggled to the Contras across the border of Nicaragua.

When the boat started circling us, Naomi sensed no danger. Thinking she should be friendly, she stepped out of the cockpit.

When she was greeted with whistles and cat calls she made a hasty retreat.

A young soldier boarded Dan's boat, which was easier, because their triple hulls keep them relatively level. He asked Dan in English, "Do you have any drugs?"

He apparently wanted some for his own use. There was no inspection.

Since we were sailing at about 6 knots healing, heeling at a 15 to 20 degree angle, they didn't try to board Destiny.

Later another small patrol boat showed up, crammed with eight or ten soldiers armed with guns. Despite the guns, they did not appear to be dangerous. Throughout it all, we had no apprehensions. Amazing Grace!

There were no patrols once we entered Nicaraguan waters.

Beggars and Food Shortage

Stopping at Corintos, on the west coast of Nicaragua, we met with Bob and Myra Trolese, the missionaries sent there by GO in Eureka. After that we would continue on through the Panama Canal to Bluefields on the east coast.

When we arrived in Corintos we met a man standing on the street corner holding a huge Iguana lizard he had killed that he was trying to sell. It was at least 18 inches long.

"What do people use them for?" I asked.

He seemed surprised I would have to ask, "Soup," he replied. To Americans that seems inconceivable, but in a country as poor as Nicaragua, food is scarce. I recalled eating alligator in Brazil.

We encountered more evidence of poverty when we went shopping in a large tent market. As Claude and I were shopping I was approached by a 14-year-old boy begging for money. I gave him some coins and asked him about himself.

His name was Carlos, and he lived with his mother in the country. He said he had to get up at 3:00 am in order to walk to town in time for the market to open. His mother sent him out to beg.

I wanted to help him, but I knew if he had a personal relationship with Jesus God would help him and his mother. I read a Chick comic tract to him, in Spanish of course. He very quickly got the point that we need to accept Jesus to be saved.

Claude and Naomi Kerr

"We need to tell *everybody* about this!" he exclaimed.

"Yes, we do!" I was so pleased with his response. "But first you need to do this yourself," and I continued to read until we came to the prayer to accept Jesus personally.

I didn't realize that little ears were listening to the story all around us. When I said I would pray with him, they seemed to appear from nowhere and joined us. They gladly joined hands and repeated the prayer one phrase at a time after me.

The Effects of Communism

We stopped at San Juan del Sur before leaving Nicaragua. We could see the effects of Communism there for the first time. As we entered the harbor we were surrounded by huge military ships flying the Russian flag that were also tied up to the docks. We were reassured by knowing President Violeta Chamorro had replaced the former, Communist president, and that she was democratic and friendly with the United States.

There we met Hazel and Murray Switzer, who we first encountered in Alcapulco on HMS Destiny. He was a CEO for Mattel Toys in Canada. HMS stands for "His Majesty's Service." All British warships have this insignia.

"This is only temporary insanity for me," Murray said. "I need to head up the east coast to Canada and work at my new position with Mattel."

The Yorks were in more of a hurry to get to Bluefields. They felt they had to get back to work after taking a year off. We didn't plan to go back to work, since Claude had a retirement income. We wanted to stop and visit some of the beautiful harbors in Costa Rica, as Americans were welcome in that democratic country.

Our next Nicaraguan port was San Juan del Sur. Claude was encountered by a man who inquired if he were Russian. No one bothered Murray. He had limited interest in us, and let us go. We found a sidewalk café where we got a cup of coffee. At the table next to us four big Russian soldiers were drinking vodka.

Walking through town, we passed a school that was closed and rundown. I went to a barber who gave haircuts in his home.

After we left Corintos we sailed about five miles offshore and we were invaded by a swarm of bees. Naomi went below and handed me a magazine to swat them and disappeared, leaving me to fight this battle alone. Violent soul that I guess I am, I must have killed at least 100 bees.

Other cruisers told us later that the bees wanted to swarm, and they seemed to gather on all the boats in our procession. I don't know why they were trying to make a new home five miles out on the ocean hanging from the booms of moving boats!

As we trolled we caught a 36" Dorado, the best eating fish in the region. When they are alive, in the water, they have shimmering golden colors This explains the Spanish name, Dorado, which means golden. When brought on deck they rapidly change to a dull grey.

It was only about 150 miles to Costa Rica. It felt so good to be in a relatively stable country, one of the most stable in the world, and a stopping place for many cruisers. Our first anchorage was at Bahia Ft. Elena where we tried out a wind generator we had bought used. It whirred so loudly and furiously in the strong wind that we soon took it down, with much labor, from the mast.

We heard strange roaring sounds from the jungle. Later we found out they were the howling monkeys. The Yorks had stopped at the same place before we got there, and when we contacted the them by radio they told us they had ventured ashore to explore. When they got out of the dingy, they heard the roaring and ran back, jumped in the boat, and raced back to the Gold Eagle.

"We didn't know what that was, but we didn't want to stay and find out!"

When we arrived at Playa de Coco we filled our tanks with diesel. When we left the wind had picked up and was right on our nose.

"We don't have to do this!" we decided, and turned back and waited for better weather. We didn't have access to weather information or forecasts, so we had to be our own weather man. Usually it worked, but not always.

We were soon to find this out.

Destiny gets a jolt!

It happened on a lovely sunny morning after a night at sea. Claude had just gone to sleep while I took the morning watch. I prepared a bowl of granola and sat down in the cockpit to eat while the autohelm kept the course. The water was choppy with whitecaps, and porpoises were playing, jumping out of the water and swimming alongside.

I decided to go below and get the camera to take pictures of the porpoises.

Suddenly the wind gave the sail a sharp jerk, and the block holding the it broke, releasing the hefty 25 foot wishbone boom that holds the bottom of the sail to swing wildly across the cockpit, stopping violently with a crash as it reversed direction to crash again on the other side.

Claude leapt into the cockpit yelling, "Get me a line!" I was shaking when I opened the locker beneath the seat asking, "which one?"

"Any one!" he snapped.

I grabbed a big coil of rope and he lashed down the boom. I hauled Claude up the mast to replace the block.

For three days we motored, too shaken to hoist the sail.

After several more stops along the coast we stopped at Puntarenas, Costa Rica, where a wide river accommodated many anchored sailboats. It was June 1, 1990.

I had a delayed reaction

"Lets do some sightseeing while we're here," Claude said, "San Jose, the capital city of Costa Rica is not too far, we can take a bus and go there today."

I really didn't feel like making the trip. I didn't know why, but I just had an uneasy feeling. We went ashore, tied up the dingy, and walked to the bus depot.

A bus was getting ready to leave, so I got on to look for seats while Claude bought tickets. There were vacant seats, but each one had something on it, a gum wrapper, or a piece of paper. I did not know if that meant the seat was reserved.

Maybe it was a sudden attack of culture shock, or maybe it was a delayed reaction to the stresses of winds and waves, but I broke into a hysterical emotional attack, sobbing uncontrollably. Claude took me to a bench outside where I kept crying while he found a bus with two seats. We got on, but I couldn't help making a scene as I continued to cry.

A kind woman came to me with a little carton of milk in an attempt to comfort me.

Finally I said, "I don't feel like going to San Jose today."

Claude did not understand my behavior, in fact I didn't either. I am glad that men do not have the emotions we women have. About a week later we did take the awaited trip to San Jose my outburst was now a distant memory.

Dan York had already stopped at Puntarenas before we arrived. Linda continued traveling to Bluefields by land. She boarded a bus, and in two hours arrived at the Managua airport in Nicaragua. The Trolese's missionary children picked her up for a two week visit. Meanwhile Dan and his son, Tom, sailed Gold Eagle the remainder of the trip. It was a good thing Linda was not with them on the passage. A fierce gale hit them.

"I was sure thankful we had the droug," said Dan. A droug is a Parachute like anchor. It was needed to slow them down and keep them safe.

Meanwhile, I went looking for Magelina's parents. She had given us their address when we met her on Carlos' boat in Puerto Vallarta. She asked us to visit them when we arrived. Her father was a fisherman. They had 13 children and about 50 grandchildren. To get to their house you negotiated a 2X12" plank across a stretch of water where bits of garbage and trash floated.

Magdalena's parents were Christians, and eager to have us return to meet some of their other children. We did come back, and I brought my flannel board and told a Bible story. Some of them admitted they had stopped serving the Lord. We helped them renew their commitments.

We hired Manuel, a Costa Rican mechanic, to work on the engine, which was still giving us problems. Claude had gone ashore, and I was left in the cabin alone with Manuel and an assistant. I strongly felt the presence of the Holy Spirit, and got out my autoharp. With all the moisture, It was a miracle that it stayed in tune all the while we were at sea. On this occasion God's Spirit was with the instrument and my voice. I sang every Spanish worship song I knew and English ones as well.

"*La musica...*," I heard Manuel breathe to his companion. I could tell it really got to him, so invited him to stay for dinner.

"Many Americans have invited me to eat with them in restaurants, but never on their boats," he said. He was touched by our friendship.

Over time grime and moss collects on boats. They need the bottom scraped and painted every two years. Up the river was a shipyard where we had it done cheaper than at home.

An American teenage girl was there visiting her boyfriend, who was cruising and wanted her to join him. I invited her to come aboard Destiny for a visit.

"How do you like Costa Rica?" I asked.

"I hate the mosquitoes!" she exclaimed. Thinking I would like to direct her towards God, I told her that mosquitoes didn't appear until after Adam sinned, and insects and weeds were part of the curse that sin brought on the earth.

"Mosquitoes are of the *devil!*" she replied with even more emphasis.

"My grandmother talks like you," she said. I was glad that she had a grandmother praying for her, and I also prayed she would go home and not stay with a man she was not married to.

I felt hesitant to leave Puntarenas. It seemed that God was moving there, and He wasn't finished yet. But Claude didn't see it that way. He felt the boat was ready, and wanted to go. I wish we had remembered to pray together about this decision but, overlooking this major need, we weighed anchor, and started off motoring across the bay. Half way across the engine quit!

Psalm 32:9 came to me:

"Do not be like the horse or mule,

"Which have no understanding,

"Which must be harnessed with bit and bridle,

"Else they will not come near you."

I was glad we were going back. When we arrived I went ashore to a place where an American had a makeshift yacht club. There at a table was Manuel!

"I have been looking for you," he said. "I got my car fixed, and I want to take you and your husband to church Sunday evening."

I gave a silent cheer, "Yeah, God!"

That evening he came with his six-year-old son and guitar, picked us up and drove us to the church he had not attended for 10 years. The people were very happy to see him return, and he joyfully played his guitar with the worship team. A woman preacher preached on the very subject that we love the most, on how God is restoring his church to what it was in the beginning.

Magdalena had a daughter, six, and son, five, who were living with her parents. The evening we were there the grandmother was putting them to bed. They cried, and I could sense their grief at being separated from their mother and father, whoever he was. Later Magdalena returned home and came to visit us on the boat. She brought the children with her. My heart went out to them as I felt the pain in their hearts.

"Do you know how much God loves you?" I asked the children. They nodded, and I continued, "He loves you so much that he sent his only son to take away your sins. He loves you so much he died in your place so that you could be God's children, too! Would you like to ask him to come into your lives?"

Their eyes lit up this time as they nodded enthusiastically. After they repeated a prayer to invite Jesus into their lives and hearts they opened their eyes, and I saw the smiles that showed Jesus was now inside and healing their broken hearts. They had true joy shining from their faces.

Central America is known in the cruising circles for its violent thunder and lightning storms. "When it rains it pours," is certainly true of this part of the world. We saw some tremendous lightning storms in Brazil as well.

In the kitchen in Brazil small streaks of light would come through the window and hit the refrigerator. One time Grant came through the gate from school immediately after lightning had struck the chain link fence in the side yard, bouncing along the top. In another storm Naomi was on the phone when lightning came through the phone line, giving her a shock that caused her to drop the phone.

We were the only boat sailing through a rain storm so heavy that visibility was less than 200 feet. No buddy boats were with us. Claps of thunder came at the same time as the flash of lightning, indicating the lightning is striking less than 1,000 feet away. We disconnected the radio and anything else we could, and prayed. Yet we were not anxious, but laughed about the 53 foot lightning rod on our boat, our aluminum mast!

We were glad that we had invested in a grounding plate that was attached to the keel. It was supposed to keep the lightning further than one mast length from the boat. Whether God used the grounding device or not, he kept us and our equipment safe. The year before, seven boats all had their electronics blown out in a lightning storm in the same area.

Even though there were no other boats with us, we knew that God was there. When we read the Bible we made special note that *God* is the one who directs the lightning, sends the wind out of his storehouses, is greater than the waves of the sea, and brings ships into their desired haven.

We stopped at a convenient anchorage as we sailed down the coast of Costa Rica. We were the only cruising boat, but we anchored and went ashore. A ranger greeted us with the news it was a national park and that boats were not allowed overnight. Claude told him that he wouldn't be able to get to the next anchorage before dark, pleading with him to let us stay. He referred us to his boss. When we approached them at the ranger station, they made no comment, and we stayed until the next day. In the morning we weighed anchor and continued sailing. By that time we were no longer sailing south, but southeast. On a map one can see that the Panama Canal is directly below Miami. This means that we had sailed south almost to the equator, but east almost 3,000 miles as well.

Claude tells about the passage to Golfito

We did fine during the day, but during the night the wind stopped, and so did our engine.

We were ten miles from shore, and I didn't think we could drift that far by morning. While I was on watch we drifted at the rate of one mile per hour south, the direction we wanted to go. We were used to always keeping watch at night, but I decided I was going to bed. Naomi, who is more conscientious than I, was indignant, "Somebody has to stand watch!" she exclaimed.

I explained why I had decided it wasn't necessary in this situation, and went to bed. She watched a little while, then came back to bed as well.

The next morning, we got up, refreshed, and found we had drifted 7 nautical miles southeast in six hours. Of course! The Holy Spirit was our Ghost Pilot!

However, we wanted to reach Golfito that day, and since the wind didn't come up, I just got into our little eight-foot Des-Tiny, tied her securely to the side of big Destiny, started up the little two horsepower outboard, and off we went at 1 or 2 knots an hour.

Naomi, not satisfied with that, radioed ahead to Patti Payne, who she had already met on the cruisers' radio net. Patti was already anchored at the Jungle Club, a boat basin across the bay from Golfito.

"We'll come right out and give you a hand!" she said. She and a friend came out in a big dingy with a powerful outboard and towed us to the Jungle Club in one hour.

The couple who owned the Jungle Club were former cruisers, who decided to settle down in Costa Rica. They bought a small vanilla plantation. That didn't seem to be the right vocation for cruisers like them. Instead they turned their energies towards developing an anchorage for travelers like us.

A palm thatched building housed a small restaurant where the wife produced great American food, including homemade bread and hamburger buns. They had laundry facilities for our use as well.

Golfito, which means "little gulf" was the site of a huge American Chicita banana plantation. All the buildings and a large dock were still there. We asked what caused them to close it down. They told us that when the Costa Rican workers went on strike for higher wages the company simply pulled out. That must be how they keep the prices of bananas down for us in the United States.

Near the anchorage a river emptied from the jungle growth. We decided to take Des-Tiny and go up the river. Usually there would be a tropical rain in the afternoon, so we brought a little yellow parasol, the only umbrella we had. Before we could make it back the rain began. We both huddled under the parasol.

"Look, we aren't the only ones out here." Naomi said, peering into the heavy rain. "There are three men paddling a canoe."

As we drew closer, we were able to see it was actually three pelicans paddling along in single file.

When we got back to the anchorage we knocked on the hull of our neighbor's boat. The wife peered out at us then disappeared inside.

The next day she said, "I thought it was the African Queen!", referring to the movie by that name starring Humphrey Bogart and Kathryn Hepburn in their older years. We were about the same age as they were.

I could say the Jungle Club was my favorite anchorage, but there are many other favorites, like one uninhabited tropical island where we swam ashore and enjoyed mangos from a huge tree.

Adventures in Panama

When we reached Panama we visited a bay called Bahia Honda. They don't make Honda cars there, but it is an island on a bay inhabited by 35 people. The first place we dropped anchor didn't suit me because of the rocky bottom. We hailed two boys in a dugout canoe and told them we were looking for an anchorage with 20 feet of water and a sandy bottom. Telling us to follow them, they showed us to their own village. It was a perfect anchorage. There were six or eight rough houses with palm thatched roofs.

The children of the village paddled out to greet us on whatever they had that would float, even a piece of Styrofoam. They brought bunches of bananas to trade for whatever we could give them. We had put in a good supply of powdered milk to give away, and traded with that. One mother came out with a crying baby asking for milk.

Besides the powdered milk I traded fishing line and hooks to the boys. Usually they didn't have anything to trade. One boy had a rock, "This is all I have," he said. I accepted it, and I became very attached to that rock. It is my pet rock. It is about eight inches long, and has been shaped as a tool. I like to think of it as a primitive axe

Another woman came and asked for shoes. Unfortunately Naomi didn't have any to spare.

"Tomorrow is Sunday," Naomi said. "Do you think the people here would like us to have a Sunday School?"

"They would like that," she answered. "There are sick people here. Two weeks ago a girl died. They would like you pray for them."

Naomi and I prayed about what to teach, and we both felt that God wants to bring people out of spiritual darkness and send them out as missionaries to other nations. He wants to call third world people to fulfill the destinies planned for them.

Naomi took her easel and flannel board and we brought New Testament Bibles in Spanish, along with some of the pencils from our school supplies. With great anticipation we went ashore Sunday morning.

Everyone gathered around. The story that Naomi chose was about Jesus calling fishermen as his disciples. The men there were all fishermen. After the story, I preached and made an appeal to them to accept Jesus.

Of all the people there the person that appeared to be the most moved was an 18-year-old boy. The expression on his face was one of longing to be used of God. We went to his house after people began to leave. After chatting a bit I prayed for him personally, asking that God would lead him. Before we left he was the last one to visit Destiny. We wished we could have taken him with us.

An elderly lady with a fresh bandage on her leg asked us to pray for her.

"A dog came right in my house and bit me!" she said. Most of the houses had no doors, being very open to keep them cool. We prayed against infection and rabies.

A few of the children took us down jungle trails and showed us all the houses. The houses were not made of finished lumber, but limbs of trees. They had no furniture, but sometimes they hung burlap sacks from long ropes attached to the rafters for seats. There was a baby in one home in one of these hammock beds. Older sisters push him to swing in a wide arc. He couldn't fall out, and slept just fine.

The gulf of Panama is full of beautiful islands and warm tropical waters. It is an ideal cruising area, too, because hurricanes do not hit that far south, and the boatyard in Puntarenas is a short distance to the north.

The only anchorage we did not like was Ensenada Benao, just east of Punta Benao. We anchored near a float marked with the name of a laboratory. On shore were several large modern buildings, and on the radio we heard people speaking in English. A high powered boat came out and circled us a couple of times while two American men frowned at us from the cockpit. All together, we were made to feel uncomfortable and unwelcome. We left there as soon as possible.

We were now approaching the Panama Canal, and were very close to our destination, Bluefields, on the east Coast of Nicaragua.

Hooray! The Panama Canal!

Arriving at the entrance to the Panama Canal was a thrilling milestone in our trip. It had taken us close to a year to get this far, as we had traveled 4,610 nautical miles, or 5,305 statute miles. We had been under engine power only 650 hours. The rest of the time the wind was our power.

As we were entering the westerly end of the canal we crossed the bow of an anchored freighter. On its bow was the name "Destiny." I got on the radio and called the captain in the usual way that captains address one another on the radio,.

"Destiny, Destiny, this is your little brother, Destiny."

"Well hello, little brother," answered a friendly voice. "Bon voyage to you!"

We anchored near Balboa Yacht Club, port of entry at the city of Balboa, and the west end of the canal. There we went through immigration and customs. We also had to have our boat measured in preparation for going through the canal.

Conditions in the Canal Zone were quite different from that of the islands and coastland of the rest of Panama. It was still in turmoil, since President Noriega had just been captured by American military for his role as a drug lord.

The rest of the country was peaceful, but it was dangerous for Americans to be on the streets of the canal zone. We made the canal passage on the passenger freighter we took to Brazil in 1970 and it went smoothly. However, in 1979 President Jimmy Carter made a treaty with Panama to turn the canal zone back to their control.

Since then, according to Americans who work there, there have been major problems in maintenance. For example, the fleet of tugboats given them by America were soon inoperable. One engine blew up because the oil had not been changed. When asked why they did not use the 50 gallons of oil reserve that was included with the boats, their cavalier answer was, "Oh, we sold it."

There was a railroad that ran the 35 mile stretch from the Pacific to the Atlantic. We decided to take a ride one day, just to see the country. We went to the station and joined other prospective passengers who were waiting for the train, which never arrived. In questioning a Panamanian who was waiting, we discovered it had not run for days. The people would come every day in hopes that it would come, so apparently at times it did show up.

Four line handlers are required besides the captain or helmsman. We needed three more besides Naomi, so we went to the military base. No one had leave, and we were about to give up.

Just in time I happened to run into two college students from New Zealand traveling the world on a low budget during their summer break. These young men were thrilled to get a free trip on a sailboat to see the canal. We only had to pay one local line handler.

The Panamanian government official who came to measure our boat was a young man, and we always enjoy meeting young people from any country. His job was to estimate the weight of boats in order to set and collect the fee. For some unknown reason they call it "measuring."

"Is it true that private citizens are allowed to carry automatic weapons in America?" he asked. He explained that he always carried a gun in his car for protection. I told him that if he believed in God he would give him all the protection he needed.

"My wife is a Christian," he said, "but I'm not." Nevertheless, he accepted my offer of prayer.

"Lord, please deliver him from the fear in his heart." I prayed.

He opened his eyes to stare at me. "You prayed just exactly what I needed!" he exclaimed.

"That is what the Bible calls a 'word of knowledge,' and it is only one of the gifts God the Holy Spirit gives us," I told him.

On the morning set for our canal passage a woman official boarded the boat. She was to be our pilot. Another pilot was assigned to "Reliance," an American sailboat rafted side by side with us. We dropped bumpers into the water to keep the hulls from damaging each other, then lashed the two together.

Descending in locks we reached the Atlantic. Notice how the sail is cradled by lines hung from the wishbone boom.

We could have gotten by with two line handlers, one on the bow and one on the stern, to throw lines to the dock workers, since the other side was secured to "Reliance." The students took control and did a great job.

We went through a series of locks, lifting us up 85 feet to the level of Lake Gatun from the Pacific. Another series lowered us down to the Atlantic side. Although our boys did a good job, the Panamanian government employee on in one of the locks delayed showing up. Then a man came running, with a card hanging around his neck by a string, and grabbed our line as it was thrown to him.

When we got to the lake we had to motor for about 25 miles and follow the channel. At this point our engine stopped.

"How about letting us sail through the lake?" I asked the pilot. "That way we can get through the locks in one day rather than two."

We thanked God she allowed us to sail, and we arrived at the Panama Canal Yacht Club anchorage in Cristobal in time for dinner. The hired man went ashore, but we invited the young men to stay for dinner and spend the night aboard. We remembered from our trip through the canal in 1970 that it was not safe in the city at night. In 1970 our friend from first class went ashore alone and was mugged and his wallet stolen.

The Panama Canal Yacht Club was not like American Yacht Clubs. The night we arrived we had to anchor outside the pier. Some clothes that Naomi washed and hung out to dry on the deck during the night were stolen.

We cruisers had a potluck dinner under a palm roof at the club. We motored to the docks in Des-Tiny, and tied it securely to a cleat. During the potluck there was a tropical downpour, and when we went to get our dingy we found it was swamped and the outboard ruined.

Later we got a berth at a dock. The first person to come and get acquainted was Carmen from *Alaskan*. She explained she was a correspondent for a Latitude 38, a boating magazine, and wanted to interview us as having arrived at the Panama Canal. Her husband, Mac, was a retired career marine.

They had been there during the American invasion, called "Just Cause" by the military. The "cause" was to capture President Noriega to stop him from shipping illegal drugs to the United States. Mac gave us quite a different eye witness account.

The American media had reported that 2,000 casualties resulted from the "invasion", making the United States look bad.

"It was a surgical strike," Mac explained. The military only attacked the police headquarters to capture their man. There were no civilian casualties from the operation.

"The casualties reported by the news media were not from the American operation. Noriega's intelligence had found out what was planned, and the day before his men went to all the bars in town and gave men a shirt and gun, instructing them that when the Americans came to go out and make trouble.

"The bar patrons gladly did what he told them, looting all the shops and taking whatever they wanted. Of course, the shopkeepers defended their stores, and as a result there were many casualties."

"The next day the streets were knee deep with the empty boxes of all the merchandise that was stolen," his wife added.

That explained why there were armed military patrolling the aisles of the supermarkets watching for shoplifters, as well as at the entrance of banks. The taxi drivers doubled as guards for American shoppers.

I went to town on foot one time with Mac and felt quite safe after he pointed out a man across the street, "One time he tried to rob me, and I hit him with my umbrella and knocked out some of his teeth. He won't bother us."

One of the benefits of being in Cristobal was the tax free store. There we were able to save money on a new outboard to replace the one that had been swamped.

Naomi tells about a friend

I wanted to use the women's restroom at the yacht club one morning, but it was locked. I came back every 15 minutes, and it was still locked. I couldn't imagine how anyone could take that long! Later I found out who it was. I was in the laundry room washing clothes, when the young Panamanian lady who worked in the government customs office came in. She asked me a question, "What do you do when you have a big problem?"

"I pray!" I answered without hesitation.

"My name is Matilde. I am a Christian, too," she responded, "and I need a place to pray. The only place I have is the restroom. Could I come on your boat and pray?" she asked.

"Of course you can!" I exclaimed, "and I will pray with you."

She came to the boat, and told me there was going to be a revival meeting in town. She had been praying, asking God to heal her nine year old son of an injury he got while riding his bicycle. We prayed together for his healing, and then she invited us to come to the meeting. She was an altar worker.

Later she invited us to her church's Sunday service.

It was children's' Sunday, and the children sang, "Father Abraham." American children march as they sing this song. There in Panama, singing in Spanish, it is transformed into a Caribbean dance, which us adults enjoyed watching as much as the kids enjoyed dancing.

Answer to the Yorks Prayer

While we were in Panama we contacted Dan York on the single side band radio. He had arrived in Bluefields. Tom returned to the States, and Linda was with him on the Gold Eagle, tied up to the Red Cross dock.

"We got our baby!" he announced. A little girl, 21 months old, was brought to the home of Ed Jaentzschke, pastor of the Verbo Church, by her mother, who asked if they could find a home for her. Later her grandfather came.

"Her twin brother is healthy, but she is sick," he said. We don't have enough food, and I am afraid she will die, like one of her sisters did."

"We asked if we could take her to the boat, and we were able to nurse her back to health. We are going to adopt her. We named her Kadi, after her grandmothers Kathryn and Diane."

A British red cross nurse arrived at the dock at just the right time to give medicine for Kadi, but the love they showed her was even more instrumental to her recovery

There are many blessings for obedience, and this was a prime example. They obeyed God's calling to go to help the people of Nicaragua, and he blessed them with the desire of their hearts!

Claude and Naomi Kerr

A blessing for obedience in going with the gospel! Dan and Linda with Kadi in Bluefields, Nicaragua.

Kadi lived in Managua with a family in the Trolese's church until the paperwork was finished for her adoption. Dan brought her home in time for her third birthday. Her new extended family showered her with presents and lots of love.

After she graduated from High School Dan and Linda took her to Nicaragua to meet her birth parents.

She said, "When I met my twin brother, I felt like something that had been missing in me came back together. Even though he couldn't speak English and I couldn't speak Spanish, we talked. I can't explain how.

"I have never had a boyfriend, so it was strange for me when he sat close to me and held my hand."

Kadi met her birth family for the first time on a trip to Bluefields. Here she and her twin brother Jim, celebrate their 21st birthdays.

She came home and became a student at the School of Ministry at Bethel Church in Redding, California. This congregation, pastured by Bill Johnson, has gained national and world recognition because of healing miracles that happen there.

Our Destiny

We were eager to get to Bluefields, now that we were on the Atlantic side, but were advised by experienced cruisers not to go yet, as it was August. Hurricane season lasts through September. Hurricanes don't often hit as far south as Nicaragua, but there was an exception two years before when they were hit by a devastating tropical storm.

Disappointed, we sat in the boat talking about what we might do while we waited.

"We could visit the San Blas Islands. They're south of here," I suggested.

"...or we could fly home and visit our kids," Naomi said.

We flew back and got our pickup and camper that were parked at our niece Kathy's house near Riverside. What a blessing to have wheels. We had a great visit with our family for three months, then returned to Miami.

God was blessing us at every turn. When we were waiting for our flight in Miami the woman at the desk called us over and said there had been two cancellations on first class, "Did we want them?" Wow! It was the only time we ever got to fly first class!

We were blessed again when we had to go through customs at the airport on the west coast in Panama, carrying with us gear for the boat, including two solar panels. An American military official who handled customs for the U.S. Army personnel got us through with only a $10 charge. Thank you Jesus!

We needed to get a taxi to take us and all our gear to Cristobal, which was only 35 miles away. Taxi drivers crowded around us. They appeared to have agreed on one price, because no one would offer any less. Remembering our experience with taxis earlier in Balboa, we thought it should have been lower. Then one man stepped forward and offered a lower price. We took his taxi, and loaded our luggage into his 1960 Chevrolet station wagon amid much commotion as the rest of the drivers protested.

Later we found out that our driver was giving up his favorite meal to make the trip. For that reason he drove like a madman, hurtling along a two lane road lined by banana trees on both sides. It was a dark, moonless night. Periodically, the headlights went out. Whenever this happened he would reach down under the dashboard as he drove and jiggle some wiring. Naomi and I started praying silently, "Lord, you have more plans for our lives, and we want to live!"

"Its awfully quiet back there," the driver said.

"We're praying," we said. After that he drove more carefully. We call that respect for God.

It was then he told us his wife had promised chicken soup, his favorite food, for dinner. I felt sorry for him, so I paid him what all the other drivers had demanded. That made him happy.

On November 17th we felt it was safe to head for Bluefields. The wind was fair, about 15 knots, and ideal for us. We were making about five knots per hour. When we were about 130 miles on our course the GPS went out and we had no means of navigation other than the compass.

We went by "dead reckoning" from then on, using the navigational chart and the compass. It would have helped to know speed and direction of currents to calculate our course, but we didn't have any information for that part of the world. We had 300 miles to go. We went about 100 miles and our engine stopped for good. Now we felt like the navigators of old, like Columbus. In fact, we were crossing some of the same waters on which he sailed.

As I look back on that time, I can see how God gave us peace in the situation. We had an advantage over Columbus because he was in uncharted waters, whereas we had a chart. Our knot log showed us how far we had come, and with the chart we could tell when we should see land. After sailing three days and nights, we saw land. We anchored behind a rock for the night because there were many reefs in the area near shore.

The next morning there was not a breath of wind. We wanted to get started, but since the engine was not working we prayed God would send an angel to help us.

The angel he sent was a strapping young black man and his father in an outboard. They stopped on their way to work as fishermen. We asked if they would tow us out where we could get some wind. The son climbed aboard and grabbed the wheel, his grin flashing very white teeth in contrast to his very black face. They towed us six miles north opposite Punto Mono, or, as our helmsman translated it in his Caribbean English, *"Mohn key*

Point". Many of the people on the east coast of Central America are English speaking since the days of English pirates.

While he was with us we learned that his mother would not let him go to Bluefields to school after the third or fourth grade. "She was afraid they would put me in the army," he explained.

At Punto Mono we picked up the wind. It was blowing toward us, and without a motor we had to tack back and forth toward our destination. Our sailing directions showed El Bluff as the entry point to Bluefields, and indicated it would be a red rock bluff. We sighted a red bluff at the end of the day, but it was not El Bluff. Anchoring behind it, we prayed for wind. In the morning, however, not a breath of wind was blowing. Again we asked God to send help.

As we stood on the bow praying, a flashing white object began to move towards us from land.

"Is that our angel?" I asked. As it drew closer we saw the sun had reflected off a white outboard which pulled up and stopped by us. Again we asked the fishermen for a tow out to where we could catch some wind. They obliged, and we threw them our prized lure in exchange, since they refused money.

"When we come back this evening we will check and see if you need help," they said in parting.

As we continued sailing south we saw a red bluff. We were very expectant, but that was not it. We continued expecting, and there was another, but that was not it either. I was so disappointed that I decided to take a nap.

"I'm tired of looking for red bluffs! That's all there is around here," I told Naomi, and went below adding, "Tell me when we get there."

I could always depend on Naomi to be faithful in situations like that.

It seemed like no time had passed when she yelled, "Here it is!"

"I'll bet!" I replied, but it actually was! We entered the outer harbor and anchored, then the customs officials came aboard.

"What are you going to do with that case of tuna?" he asked, pointing at a box under the companionway ladder.

"We are bringing it to help the people," we replied. This response pleased him.

A friendly Nicaraguan we met at the entry office gave us a tow for two miles up the channel to the Red Cross dock where Dan had tied up. The Yorks had stayed there for six months, but it was necessary for them to get home, since they were running out of money and didn't have a retirement income like we did.

No sooner had we anchored than an outboard came up and a smiling Ed Jaentschke jumped out. We had heard a lot about this man from the Yorks. He was pastor of the Verbo Church. He brought with him a slender black man who he introduced as Harry, a good mechanic. What a welcome! God knew what we needed. I told him about our engine trouble.

"I'll fix it for you!" he assured me.

He came to the boat the very next day and began working. It was more than he could diagnose on his own, and the next day he brought his cousin along, and he kept working on it for a several weeks. No one else was able to find the problem, but these men in a third world country, one of the poorest places in the world, came up with the answer!

Harry discovered the reason for the engine continuously heating up. All the water passages were plugged up with what looked like crushed oyster shells. They must have been sucked up when the previous owner backed into an oyster bed.

"We'll have to clean the water passages and get a new valve and valve spring," he said.

We didn't know where we could get the parts, since everything was scarce in Nicaragua. As Harry left I gave him and his cousin each a can of tuna.

The next day Harry thanked me saying," That was the first meat my family has had in two months!"

We Americans just don't know what it is like to go without. In Nicaragua, if you need a guitar string you probably won't be able to find one. If you could find toothpaste, there may be only three or four tubes in the store. There was no big selection of anything.

Pastor Ed introduced me to Jorge, who he said could take care of all my contacts with the government office so I could get a visa. He also made a trip to Managua, the capital near the East Coast, and found the parts for the engine.

I paid Harry and his helper a very good salary compared with what was normal for Nicaragua at that time.

"How about you preaching on the radio this Sunday?" Ed asked me.

"I would like to, but my Spanish isn't very good!" I explained.

He laughed and said, "Don't worry, the people here understand English!"

Sunday morning he took me to the radio station. When I sat down at the desk, took the microphone and began to speak everyone left me alone. I was supposed to continue for 30 minutes. This was my first experience of preaching on the radio! All I could do was ask God to help me. He did, and I did it.

When the Communists came in from Cuba and Russia they shut down all free enterprise industry such as the fish packing plant. The only jobs available were government jobs. Poverty was evident by the few cars in town. Once two trucks and a car arrived at the intersection at the same time. There was a traffic jam, as all three drivers blew their horns contending for the right of way.

Ravages of the hurricane were still evident after two years. Winds up to 220 miles per hour destroyed 90% of the homes. The people built shacks out of the scrap lumber that was scattered about. Often you would see a bare foundation, perhaps with a toilet still in place. Many homes had outhouses. Usually they were careful not to place them uphill from a well.

Claude and Naomi Kerr

Harry's house is a small building to the left.

Jaime was a very enterprising man I befriended. He had a boat that he would take up the river to buy cattle, bringing them back to Bluefields to sell. He would tell me about the economy while we walked through town, pointing out houses that were built by people whose relatives had moved to the States and sent money back. Others were fortunate to have Church or humanitarian groups send teams to build homes for them.

Harry, the man who fixed our engine, used to have a boat, but the Sandanistas confiscated it when he refused to take political prisoners out to sea and push them overboard.

After seeing all the poverty I wanted to help somehow. I preached at the church about what the Bible says regarding work and prosperity, and offered to meet with anyone who wanted to start his or her own business. I offered some suggestions I thought of to fill basic needs in Bluefields.

The first ones to respond were Demry and Victoria, a young couple who were, like many others, were living in his parents' home with their own children as they had no income of their own. They came to the dock and Claude brought them out to the boat, one at a time. He didn't know what to do when Victoria cried from fear. We never had thought of the choppy water as a threat, but of course he got her there safely.

"I have an idea for a business of my own," Demry said. "I want to sell produce at the market. I hate having to depend on my parents. At least I would be able to put food on the table!"

I told Ed we wanted to help and gave him $300 for the church to loan to those who were starting businesses. Before they could borrow money I required them to come to classes that I held every week. Seven or eight men were faithful to come regularly.

Demry wanted $100 to start his produce stand. We suggested Ed loan him $50 to see if that would be enough, and it was. He not only built the wooden stand and stocked it with fruit, but within two months he was supporting his family. He also paid off the loan, saved an extra $100, and came dancing up the aisle to bring his tithe of 10% for the offering at church.

As for us, we were running out of cash for our own expenses. It was not wise to exchange American dollars in Nicaragua due to the monthly inflation losses, so we decided to fly to Miami, since we had other business to do there.

When we arrived at the airport in Managua I had to go into a customs office where several officials were seated at a table. They said we had to get an exit visa and that it would cost $25. The problem was we only had $15 cash left. I asked if I could charge it on my credit card, but they refused.

In the meantime, Naomi was waiting in line to board the plane. As I delayed, she began to pray, urgently reminding God that he had promised to supply all our needs in Christ Jesus.

"I'm going to Miami to get money, so I'll pay you when I get back, OK?" I told the officials. They answered with an even more emphatic "no!"

"My plane leaves in 15 minutes!" I stated firmly. They looked at each other and said the equivalent in Spanish of, "Get out of here!"

So we did catch our plane!

We went to a bank when we got to Miami, but to our surprise, none of the employees could understand English. On the street we asked directions to an English speaking bank, but the person we asked did not understand English either. I couldn't believe that in Nicaragua there were more bilingual people than in America!

After getting cash I bought some tools for Harry. Then I went to a music store to get guitar strings, bass strings, and drum sticks for Jorge to start a business. He played guitar in the church and knew there was a need for all those items.

Our return trip to Bluefields went without incident. Praise the Lord!

It was then that we were notified that our GPS, which we had sent to the factory for repair had been shipped back to Managua. Unfortunately there was a strike of all government employees so the customs office would be closed.

"I will go to Managua and I will not return until I have it!" declared Jorge. A week later he returned with our package in hand, another reason to praise the Lord! Now we had all we needed to return to the U.S. before hurricane season.

Several of us went to the local prison to preach. I was asked to do the preaching. After telling them that Jesus died in their place so they could be forgiven of their crimes, I asked if anyone wanted to ask Him into their lives. Seven men responded and we prayed with them to repent and turn their lives over to God.

Ed made arrangements to baptize them, and the next Sunday they came, accompanied by armed guards. The guards were not allowed to go into a church with guns, and sat on a wall across the street to watch. No one tried to escape.

Encounters With Teachers, Naomi

Near the Red Cross dock where Destiny was anchored was an old two-story house, which was tilted when the hurricane knocked it off its foundation. One morning as I was walking to town a woman came out that house on her way to work.

Walking along with her I asked, "Where do you work?"

"I am a teacher," she replied.

"Oh, I was a teacher," I commented. "I love children."

"Well, you have to love children to teach in Nicaragua," she said. "You can't be doing it for money, because the government only pays $100 a month, and half the time we don't get paid."

"What grade do you teach?"

"I usually teach sixth, but last year I had forty students, and I had to talk so loud I lost my voice, so I took younger children this year."

I met another teacher at a street meeting. A Youth With a Mission (YWAM) team had come and was performing a mime skit. I looked over the crowd that had gathered and I was especially impressed by the face of a barefoot woman. I joined her as she walked away. I found out her name was Marta, and like half the population, only spoke Spanish. I asked her the first question that came to my mind, "Marta, do you know anyone who loves you?"

Without any hesitation she replied, "No one!"

"Where do you sleep?" I asked

"Sometimes under a house."

"Come with me and I will take you to some people who love you."

I took her to the pastor's house. They took her in, and I gave her some Bible verses to encourage her of God's love. Overnight she seemed to be transformed by their expressions of His love together with God's promises of forgiveness from the verses I had given her. People all over town were amazed that she had been taken in by the church. At one time she had been a teacher, but became addicted to sniffing glue and led a life of prostitution.

I prayed to find out what the Lord wanted me to do in Bluefields and felt that I was there for the children. There were many children in the church. Ed asked me to train the Sunday School teachers.

There were five or six young women living with Ed and Ligia, his wife, and their two children. These girls would have been hired out by their parents or aunts as prostitutes if they had not escaped to their house for refuge.

There were also young men who lived at a farm building on a property that had been purchased for them by a church in England. These young people were the Sunday School teachers. I set up my flannel board and demonstrated how to use flannel figures to tell Bible stories. They had never seen a flannel board before, so when I invited them to experiment with the figures they put the figures in the sky or upside down, just for fun.

Nora used the flannel board I brought with the Kindergarten Sunday School class.

After we had been there for a few months I met Nora, a married lady with children of her own. She was a good teacher and felt confidant with the flannel board. One Sunday morning she did not show up to teach her Kindergarten class, and, although I was totally unprepared, I had to substitute.

God came to my rescue. I opened my mouth and he gave me a story about the Apostle Peter in the English idiom that they speak at home, before going to school where they are taught in Spanish. It is a colorful, language all their own that is ungrammatical and not taught anywhere.

Nora and I decided to have a School of Worship on Saturdays for the children. Although adults danced and sang freely at the Verbo services, I saw the children were holding back.

We planned a series of Bible story dramas about the life of King David, featuring his love of worshiping in song and dance. I wanted to offer craft activities, but had no supplies. Pondering this dilemma, I heard God's quiet voice bringing to my mind a phrase from the Bible:

"But what are these among so many?"

The context was that Jesus was about to multiply a few little loaves of bread and dried fish to feed thousands of hungry people. That is what he did for us in supplying crafts. We made banners out of scrap wood I found at the Red Cross headquarters for poles and a spare bed sheet we had aboard, rhythm instruments from empty tuna cans, and Bible figures from toilet tissue tubes and scraps of cloth.

I announced the school on the radio and children came walking from all over town. We never saw the parents, for they came on their own. The young men and women from the pastor's group were the actors and instructors. After a little encouragement, the children took front seats in the church and danced and sang during worship services.

Whenever I walked to town I noticed a stooped and wrinkled woman holding a baby who looked very malnourished. I met the mother of the baby and found that she was unable to nurse him as she was able to get very little food for herself. She lived with her mother, baby and four daughters in a makeshift home made from a sheet of black plastic extended from the crumbled remains of a house.

This single mother had no way to provide for her mother and four small children.

This enterprising woman was able to send her older girls to school by making friends with foreign visitors such as myself. I brought food to them, and other tourists she spoke to bought the girls shoes to wear to school.

"There used to be a program run by Swedish people who would give me flour to bake bread to sell, but the program ended," she said, adding with a touch of irritation, "One church minister had flour, but when it got weevils he threw it out! I could have strained the weevils out."

She had baked the bread over a charcoal fire in a wok propped up on bricks. One time she smilingly showed me a large bag of overripe tomatoes.

"A merchant at the street market gave me these!" she said. "I will make some sauce to give to my children."

Immorality and theft were also prevalent in Bluefields. When the church opened a preschool one of the questions asked of the parent was, "Are you married or living together?" If they offhandedly said, "Living together," it was accepted without further questions. One time I went to visit the mother of six children who were living with their father.

"Why haven't you ever married?" I asked.

Her face brightened with hope as she replied, "We plan to be married. I already have a dress for the wedding."

Later we were happy to learn that they had a wedding.

Once I was out after dark having a meeting with the Sunday School teachers, while Claude went to Ed and Ligia's house. Before I realized it, everyone had left and I was alone. I did not want to walk to the dock in the dark alone, so I walked to the Jaentschkes. Ed said Claude had already left, but he would give me a

The bride and groom.

ride home on his motorcycle. I should have refused, but I was afraid to go alone in the dark, so I climbed on the motorcycle behind him.

The next day I encountered the night watchman on the dock. With raised eyebrows he asked, "Where is Ed?"

Knowing what he was implying I hurriedly explained, "Last night I was at a Sunday School teachers' meeting, so he gave me a ride home."

With a sly smile he replied, "Oh, sure!"

Later I was in town shopping, and a woman looked at me knowingly asking, "Where's Ed?"

I mention this as a warning to anyone who might be in a foreign country as a missionary. Gossip flies and it is difficult to dispel rumors, especially in poverty stricken cultures where women are exploited.

Harry, who had worked on our engine, lived in a little house he had built for his family from scraps left by the hurricane. His wife took in laundry and his six-year-old son was eager to help us carry buckets of water to the boat during the dry season.

One day I went to visit and met his wife's aunt, who lived with them. The man had turned a nonworking refrigerator into an oven, and she was busily baking cakes to sell for Christmas. She ran another business on the side employing women. She gave a note to her niece.

"Deliver this message to room 13 in the hotel," she said.

When the young girl knocked on the door she found a strange man inside waiting for her. She took off running until she arrived at Ed's house. From then on she became part of the family, along with the other girls who had escaped before they could be pressed into prostitution.

Shopping in Bluefields

We had a working refrigerator in the Destiny galley when we bought the boat, but it quit working while we were in Bluefields. I found that I could live the same way as the locals. Few of them owned refrigerators. Animals would be slaughtered every evening refrigerated overnight. In the morning merchants would lay the meat out on open tables on the street.

Americans always think of flies getting on meat in the open, but I never saw flies on the meat I bought. The meat was sold out before the sun became hot. Women cooked the main meal of the day at noon, so you bought it and cooked it before it could spoil. There was also a store that sold chicken, cut up, packaged and kept in a refrigerator, just like home. It cost more than beef, but I was glad to get it.

If I didn't get out in time to buy the meat I could buy shrimp in the afternoon from boys who went out in canoes rigged with black plastic sails. They walked around the streets calling out their wares. It cost me the equivalent of 80 cents for a one pound coffee can full of shrimp of varied sizes. Of course it was in the shell and had to be peeled.

Another source of meat was sea turtles. Every Saturday fishermen would slaughter turtles measuring at least 3 feet in diameter. Townspeople would come to an open table near the water front to buy parts, while street dogs fought under the table for the scraps.

I had to learn to answer the question, "What part do you want?" If I said "meat" I got straight red meat resembling beef. Nora told me, "Food is scarce you know. We don't throw away any parts of the turtle. We even eat the intestines."

Once I bought liver, and it was the best we ever ate. The meat tasted like stew beef, once I learned to cook it like I would a stew.

There was no place to buy fish, since the packing plant had closed. It appeared there would be an improvement when an American fishing boat appeared. The fishermen wanted to help the country by providing jobs. The delays and costs of getting permits was so prohibitive that they gave away the fish they had caught, and went home.

The first week we were there I had no trouble buying fresh produce at the open air market. There were potatoes, onions, garlic, tomatoes, various other vegetables, bananas and oranges. But there were many weeks when there were only potatoes, onions and cabbage.

The diet and exercise resulted in excellent health for both of us. We both lost weight, and were strong and vigorous. My cholesterol was dangerously high when I was at home living the American lifestyle, but in Bluefields it dropped to normal.

It was getting near the beginning of hurricane season which began in June, when we would be leaving, and we still had a nice supply of pencils and crayons. I was considering giving them to the public schools when we learned that Ed and Ligia's *El Verbo* church was asked by a government official to start a school.

Ed asked me to train the teachers. The pre-school class would be the first grade to implement, with another grade level to be added each year. I brought out the math games I had with me and assembled them. I typed up playing instructions for each game. Sometimes I had problems in communication.

"What would you do if a child broke a rule?" I asked a teacher.

Her confident reply mystified me. "I would have him or his parents pay for it," she stated, matter of factly.

Moran, the assistant pastor who was sitting by, overheard our conversation. Detecting a language problem, he explained to me she was speaking of a ruler, while I was thinking of classroom rules.

The only location the church had for a school was the property where we had services. The meeting place was just like the one in Busesrias with a concrete floor and a roof, but no walls. When it rained sometimes the folks near the edge got sprinkled, but in the tropical temperature (Bluefields was only 12 degrees north of the equator) no one complained if they got wet.

Two classrooms were needed, and Claude got the idea for creating a separation.

"We have a heavy sail that we never will use," he told me. "I think we could use it for a partition. We brought it to the future *Verbo School*, and Claude nailed it to a rafter. It served very well during school hours, and could be rolled up for the services. Pastor Ed was pleased.

I got to see a little of the beginning of the new school before we were compelled to leave Bluefields. The hurricane season would begin soon, something we had become well aware of during our stay in a hurricane and war ravaged community. Besides, we were headed for Miami, notorious for hurricanes.

It was gratifying to me, after teaching in public schools in the U.S. to see the teachers and children join hands together first thing in the morning to pray and worship. The children instantly took to presenting requests to pray for parents' and their own needs. Since we left the school it has grown to include all grades with 420 students meeting in a large building of its own. One can see pictures on *www.nicaraguahope.org*.

According to the website, "Since the Verbo school is private and charges a tuition, only 112 of the 420 students can actually afford this fee. The other 72% are getting free tuition subsidized by the school because their families lack the income."

The week before we had to leave I asked some of the residents how they survived the tragedies of the 30 year civil war, hurricanes, poverty and communism.

The answer I received each time was the same, "by faith."

When I asked more specifically the response was, "Faith in God!"

In the years since our visit this trust in God and openness to Christianity has brought economic prosperity to Bluefields. We have noted that in our own lives as well. Whenever we honor him, God honors us.

When we finally said goodbye, it was with much sorrow. As we motored out the channel towards the customs office in El Bluff I gave in to an uncontrollable torrent of tears . I felt like God's Holy Spirit was grieving through me for the sufferings of the people we had grown to love. I thought of the widow woman who wanted her son to have a pair of shoes, the child who was crying pitifully because he did not have the strength to draw up a full bucket of water out from the deep well where he had been sent for water, the little girl who couldn't go to school because her mother could not pay for a uniform and books, and my spirit grieved, as it does to this day.

As we hoisted the sail and began beating into the adverse winds I felt increasingly nauseated and became ill. We had been six months on land, and I lost my "sea legs," and again I began to weep uncontrollably. The prophet Jeremiah's expression describes what I felt:

"Oh that my head were a spring of water
and my eyes a fountain of tears!
I would weep day and night for...my people."
Jeremiah 9:1

The prophet Jeremiah and I were both experiencing the emotions of God Himself toward suffering. Suffering is not his will, but is the consequence of accumulation of evil acts.

Refuge in Corn Island, Claude

The one challenge that always looms overhead, consuming my thoughts, is the requirement of avoiding hurricanes. About all we had to do, since the engine ran well and we had a working GPS, was to fill our tanks with fuel and water, stock up on food, and leave.

We did this with much sadness. It's not easy to leave a needy people you have grown to love.

When we left Bluefields our goal was to go offshore about 10 miles, then head north. That meant beating into the wind blowing from the north, towards Florida. Also we were fighting the current. After sailing the first day we saw land. It was Corn Island, 15 miles off the coast.

"I have a surprise for you!" I called to Naomi, who was seasick. "We are going to land and rest."

She said not to land for her, but I was somewhat frustrated, so we decided to pull in for the night rather than continuing our struggle.

Corn Island is part of Nicaragua. We had heard of people from Bluefields going there to look for packages of drugs thrown overboard by traffickers being apprehended by the Coastguard. Sure enough, when we went ashore a man sidled up to us and asked, "Do you want to buy some coke?"

Naomi, in her innocence, replied, "Coca Cola?"

"No!" he answered with disgust, "Cocaine!"

Before leaving we had turned in our itinerary to customs, and it did not include Corn Island.

"We will have to contact Bluefields by radio to get permission for you to leave," the customs officials asserted.

Since the ship's bottom had not be cleaned since we left, I took advantage of this delay. At first we tried diving down with snorkels to scrape. It was hard work, and finally I found a scuba diver who was looking for work.

Thinking of our trading T shirts for lobster in Bahia Santa Maria, Naomi tried bartering with him, offering him various articles. Again, like the cocaine dealer, the reaction was disdain. Money was all he would consider.

The population of Corn Island and custom officials seemed to have that kind of spirit. I went back several times trying to get permission to leave, but they claimed the radio didn't work. Finally I offered them money, and they gave us permission to leave.

We continued north up the coast. Again we were beating into the wind and in rough seas. It was very slow. Sometimes a reality in sailing. We would climb up on a large wave to the top, and then crash down on the other side. Spray would fly, hitting 30 feet up the sail.

One time we went over a wave and one of the blocks used for adjusting the sail exploded in pieces and the sail crumpled. The block was 12 feet high up the mast. It was impossible to go up in the bosun's chair in such rough weather.

We motored through the night and prayed that the weather would be better in the morning. It was a rough night. When we each got off watch we would wear earplugs to sleep. It didn't help much in deadening the crash as each wave broke, plus the sound of the engine near the berth. It was not a night for sweet dreams!

In the morning it had improved, but seas were still a little big. Nevertheless, I decided to try replacing the block. I would have to remove a cotter pin and shackle, taking the broken block off, replacing it with a new block. Finally, I had to put the parts back together. This might be simple when on solid ground, but out in a boat on a tossing sea it is a different story!

With my little 100 pound wife hoisting me up, I had to wrap my legs around the mast to keep from swinging out as the waves passed under the hull. I was able to hang on well with my legs, but once I bruised a leg. It seemed like a miracle the way all those parts quickly fit together. There was no problem at all handling the small pin. I don't think I could have done it any better if I were doing It on a workbench at home. Praise the Lord! He helps us in many mysterious ways!

The next day we rounded *"Cabo Gracias a Dios"*, meaning, "Cape Thanks be to God." We gave thanks to God, too, as Christopher

Columbus did when he named it. He had to fight the same sea conditions as we did.

Our next challenge was to navigate through many coral reefs. Columbus would not have been able to get through this area during the night, as we did. The GPS gave us our exact location on the earth's surface within 30 feet. At this writing the accuracy has improved considerably, to at most three feet. With GPS the military can hit a target as small as the front door of a building. We took GPS readings every hour during the night to stay in the center of the channel.

I remembered reading in a book, *Cruising the Caribbean*, about a good anchorage in Honduras called *Viverio Cays*. It was nothing more than a 10 foot high mound of coral offshore. It was difficult to see because it was low. However we found it easily with the GPS because we had the latitude and longitude.

It was a good sail. We were making 7 1/2 knots, about our maximum hull speed. That would be 11 mph, not fast driving a car, but maximum for a 30 foot boat. We had traveled for six days from Bluefields, so it was reason to shout, "Land ho!", or, perhaps, in this case, "Reef ho!" We were glad to drop our anchor to rest for a couple of days.

Another reason for our good spirits was an encounter with another American cruising couple who were anchored near the reef. They introduced themselves as "Joe and Moe." Their card said "Joe and Marian Dean" and their boat was named *Silent Quest*. We didn't realize how much we missed the camaraderie of the cruising community. We hadn't had it in Bluefields, a destination that does not attract cruisers, unlike the rest of the Caribbean.

Naomi was so glad to see them that she radioed immediately and invited them to come to our boat for a breakfast of French toast in the morning.

"We came here to meet friends who are bringing us some rigging to replace a broken stay," they told us.

The next day I went to hoist the anchor, but it just wouldn't come up without straining with all the strength I had to work the manual winch. When it finally came up I saw the difficulty. It had hooked a huge ball of coral and cables left there by many boats. Cables are used on conventional sailboats to fasten the mast to the deck.

Most boats carry cable cutters, but since our boat had no need of stays with its freestanding, unstayed mast, Naomi radioed and called Joe and Moe for help. They immediately came over in their inflatable dingy with a pair of cable cutters, and freed us so we could continue our passage to Florida. Our God faithfully provides what we need no matter where we go.

Favorable winds carried us north along the east coast of Mexico's Yucatan Peninsula. The winds and current were with us. We sailed at night between the mainland and the island of *Cozumel*, which I would describe as a typical tourist trap. Seeing all the buildings lit up on the island, we felt privileged to be on our own boat. Our destination was *Isla Mujeres*, where we would stay at one of the two marinas we found in Mexico.

We Pick Up Some Hitchhikers, Naomi

Migrating birds often alight on boats to rest their wings on their long flights. On this passage we picked up two little swallows who lit on the cockpit. They may have been mates. My first reaction was to capture a photo of our cute passengers.

Before I went down to get the camera one of them flew into the cabin below. When she saw me, she flew over to me and lit on my head. She did not move when I went to the companionway and handed the camera to Claude to take a photo. Later I found the other one dead among the cushions of the salon. Sadly, he never made it to land.

Headed for Florida, Claude

Arriving at Isla Mujeres, it seemed almost like coming home. The marina was full of American boats. After seven months this was only our second encounter with Americans. We went out to eat and I ordered chorizo pizza. Bad choice. It made me sick and I was miserable all night.

We were there for four days, so I did some diving to clean the bottom a little more before going on to Florida. We would have left on Saturday, but when we found out eleven boats would leave together on Sunday, we waited to join the fleet. We welcomed the opportunity to sail with this friendly flotilla, after a year of sailing solo.

Destiny's speed was a surprise to the others, as our length was only 30 feet and the others were longer. Speed is determined by the length at the waterline. Our boat's waterline was long for our size due to the shape of the hull, and our sail was very efficient. We got a late start, but within a few hours we had passed all the other boats except a forty five footer.

After we passed the western tip of Cuba, we picked up the gulf stream, a major current that flows around the tip of Florida. We were sailing 5 knots, but with the added push of the gulf stream current, we were doing 9 1/2 knots over the bottom.

As night settled in, a black cloud was coming up behind us. I prayed and started up the motor, hoping to outrun it by motor sailing. Water spouts had been reported by the U.S. National Weather Service, which we could finally pick up. A water spout is like a tornado at sea, and they cannot be seen at night. I couldn't outrun the dark cloud, but it passed over us without mishap. Again God showed us his care.

Our first American landfall was Dry Tortugas Island off the tip of Florida. The Confederates built Fort Jefferson there , but it was never used. It still stands as a pristine relic of the Civil War.

The Dry Tortugas anchorage was crowded. During the night the wind picked up, and looking outside I saw a neighboring boat drift by on our starboard side, then another one moved by on the port side. They must have been new sailors who did not know how to set their anchors.

We never drug anchor during our entire trip. I think it was because we had a good anchor rode. It was made up of a Bruce anchor one size larger than was recommended for our boat. Instead of nylon line we had all chain. The amount of chain we used was five times the depth of the water where we were anchored.

Lots of gear we brought along for emergencies was never needed, since our God was faithful to give me wisdom and protection. We had a long nylon anchor line in case we had to anchor during a hurricane. We also had a life raft, man overboard pole, and a parachute anchor for use in storms, plus a water desalinator we never used because we caught rain water.

The next morning we were told to move out of the harbor for security reasons. The Queen of England's private yacht was due to arrive. We were not as interested in trying to see the queen as we were eager to get back on American soil, so we weighed anchor and headed for Fort Myers, passing up the Keyes.

From the time we left the United States I had been praying that we wouldn't be boarded by the U.S. Coastguard, and we never were. We had heard horror stories about cruisers who were searched. Without risk of liability, they could do up to $5,000 in damage to boats when they searched for drugs.

We traveled a total of 7,187 statute miles since leaving our home port.

CHAPTER EIGHT

Helping the World in America

Bad and Good News, Naomi
As soon as we arrived in the U.S. I first phoned our son Scott. He and his family were doing well. But then I phoned Grant.

"I'm doing well after my surgery," he said.

Shocked, I asked in alarm, "What surgery?"

"Oh, you don't know? I had my thyroid removed. There was a little cancer. The doctor told me if you are going to have cancer that is the best place to get it. He assures me that they got it all."

When I hung up I remembered. On April 18th, Scott's birthday, I began thinking about Grant spending the first birthday of his life in the hospital with bronchial pneumonia. I told Claude what I was feeling.

"We need to pray for Grant!" I said. "I just started thinking about when he was a baby and was in the hospital. Maybe God is telling me he is in the hospital now!" Now I was glad we did.

After talking to Grant I prayed, "Lord, don't let there be any more cancer in his body!"

Then I heard God's voice saying, "He is earmarked."

This expression comes from the law of Moses. It refers to a Hebrew slave who, after seven years, has the right to be set free.

"*But the slave may plainly declare, 'I love my master...I would rather not go free.' ...Then his master must take him to the door and publicly pierce his ear with an awl. After that the slave will belong to his master forever." Exodus 21:5,6 NLB*

This gave me confidence that Grant had committed his life to serve God as his master, and the Heavenly Father would not allow him to suffer more cancer.

I had expected to continue traveling on Destiny to other needy places in the world, but Claude showed signs of losing the desire. We found a marina at Tarpon Springs on the west coast of Florida near a church that was started by GO.

"We have seen a lot of foreign countries, but we haven't seen our own country yet!" Claude lamented, adding, "If you have car trouble in your own country, you just pull over to the nearest garage and you can get it fixed."

Another time he looked out of the cockpit at the water and mused, "You can grow a garden on land."

I agreed, thinking of our little house in Eureka, and of Gospel Outreach, where we knew people we had grown to love. However we would not make any plans without knowing if it was God's will for us. We knew we had a calling to be missionaries, so we waited for Him to confirm our leaning toward moving ashore.

Claude's Infection and Dr. Killam

The wound that Claude had received going up the mast had become infected, probably from diving in dirty harbor water at the marina when we were at *Isla Mujeres before leaving Mexico.* I read in the *First Aid at Sea* book that one could crush a sulfur tablet to make a salve to treat such lesions. I did that, but was still worried, so I convinced Claude to see a doctor.

"Dr. Killam Is In," said the sign on the desk of the urgent care clinic. My maiden name is Killam, and seeing someone else by that name is very rare. It turned out that he came from a branch of my father's family that had settled in Canada.

"I'm going to send this to the lab," said Dr. Killam, after taking a biopsy.

I told him about my Grandfather Flint, a country doctor in Connecticut

"Do people ever kid you about your name?" I asked, thinking of the many people who joked about my name.

"Oh yes, especially when you are a doctor!"

Our Destiny

I made an appointment for myself with Dr. Killam before we left Ft. Myers.

"There were two other doctors in our family line," I told him. I had done a little research while at a Killam family reunion in Massachusetts. "They both changed their names."

"To what?" he wanted to know.

"To Stevens."

"That's weird," he replied.

At the end of my visit I was blessed when he said, "No charge, professional courtesy." He was not obligated to do this, but it is professional courtesy for doctors to treat family members of other doctors without charge.

The report came back from the lab showing Claude had a staph infection.

Back to California, Claude

It was time to have the boat hauled out to clean and paint the hull, so after we motored upriver from the port we left for California.

The doctor was reluctant to have us go without treating the staff infection, but I assured him I would be back home in a week and go to my own doctor and take care of it.

It was so hot and humid in Florida that we were glad to get away for the summer. On our trip home we attended a church near New Orleans where some of the men prayed for my leg to be healed. Some of the people offered us their Southern hospitality and invited us home for jambalaya before sending us on our way.

I went to a clinic in San Jose and the staph infection cleared up within a short time. After visiting family for a few months we returned to the marina in Tarpon Springs where we had left Destiny.

We often see evidence that God's plan for our lives, our destiny, is navigated from heaven. Everything dovetails into that plan. For example, during ten months we lived in Florida we met some wonderful people, many who have remained friends until this day.

In New Port Richie, the town next to Tarpon Springs, we went to a GO Church where new friends made us feel like part of their family. After a few months, it was announced that Jim Durkin would be visiting from Eureka to ordain elders. The Holy Spirit led us to fast and pray that God reveal his will to us through Jim. That was exactly what happened.

During the ordination service Jim went to the microphone and said, "Claude and Naomi Kerr, I want to speak to you after the service."

Approaching us after the service, he said, "I have a vision for your ministry in Eureka. Would you consider moving up and joining us there?"

That was just another confirmation of God always giving us the desires of our heart, desires that he put in our heart from the beginning. We notified the tenants who had rented our house in Eureka that they would have to move, and made plans to relocate there as soon as we could make arrangements.

Rather than sail back to California, against the wind all the way up the coast, or sell the boat in Florida at a loss, we decided to ship it back by land to the place where we bought it, and put it up for sale there. It seemed to us so many boats are sold in Florida it brings down the price.

When we were driving back to California from Florida we met a retired German couple who were vacationing in a RV. As we talked we found that we all had the same faith in God through Jesus.

We talked about our missionary trip to Nicaragua.

"You should be missionaries right here!" the husband exclaimed. "I can see there is a great need for God right here in your own country!"

This statement rang true for us. Today we have a new missionary call, to the younger generation here. Realizing we were not in touch with their generation, we began to ask God how we could remedy that. He gave us the idea of conducting a survey of young folks between the ages of 13 and the early 20s.

"We need to ask them four basic questions," Claude said. "What is your greatest need? What is your greatest fear? What is your greatest question? And What is your greatest desire?"

In the local mall and in Old Town Eureka we approached all the young people we could find, asking them the four questions. After questioning over 300 of them we realized few of them had any idea of their purpose for existing or how they would make it through life.

Dangers of nature and fear of dying or losing loved ones, lack of security because of divorce, and fear of the future affected them, even though they managed to maintain hope for some kind of happiness.

Many young people today have no knowledge of God, and no interest in finding out if he exists. Some have concluded there is no God.

We decided to illustrate how God is very real and has a purpose for each of our lives through our own experiences. We enlisted an artist to help us, and began writing small four page tracts about us and the exciting things we have done. We found the young men and women were receptive to these stories, and often eager to hear more.

Claude asked a teen aged girl, "What is your greatest need?"

With tears in her eyes, she answered, "I need a new family!"

Seeing how disillusioned they were regarding marriage and family, we wrote another brief tract, using our own marriage and family to illustrate how it can and will succeed if we follow God and his ways of doing things.

This book began as tracts, "Our Destiny" and "Perfect Storm."

Whenever we go out we have these stories in our pockets, and every young person and some older ones receive them gladly.

"Do you have a vision for your life?" I asked one young man.

Surprised, he answered, "Well….no, I don't!"

Giving him a story, I explained that there is a destiny for him, and he can find out what it is by talking to God. One of the guys gave Claude a nickname, "Papa C." The name stuck.

All of these experiences with young people we meet and our own six grandchildren, three boys and three girls who range from 15 to 28, have fueled a desire to turn it all into this book.

Scott and Laurie, our oldest son and daughter-in-law, after being married for 30 years have produced another successful marriage. Andrew, their oldest son, married Nicole, Niki to us, a young lady he met in a church's youth group street outreach. He and Niki bought a house before they married, just like Andrew's

Mom and Dad. They were both raised as Christians and maintain their faith, and both love sports.

Brandon, Scott and Laurie's middle son, is 25. He mentors 21 young people who live communally in his church's building, traveling out of town and beyond many weekends to evangelize in various communities.

Mekenzie, 15, is an honor student with a great future, and loves Jesus with all her heart. She was born in Korea, coming to join our family at the age of four months.

Alex, Grant and Debbie's oldest, is 25 at this writing. He has special abilities in art, writing and computer skills. Right now he is taking classes that earn a certificate in graphic arts. His sister Alisha is about to graduate with a BA in nutrition from Cal Poly, while Lauren, Grant's youngest, is in Honolulu majoring in botany at Hawaii State University.

More Trips to Foreign Lands

God has not stopped sending us out. In 1995 we attended a School of Divine Healing with Randy Clark in Albany, Oregon. "I am looking for a team of 50 to go to Brazil with me as a prayer team," he announced.

We immediately volunteered to go. The team left September 10th, 2001. When we arrived at the Rio de Janiero Airport we heard that the twin towers had been attacked in New York City. We went ahead and visited eight meeting sites and 10,000 healings and deliverances were reported.

By healing the sick and casting out demons we got vengeance against the devil for what he did to our country. What's more, what he did in America worked together for good, by producing much patriotism. Brazilians expressed great sympathy for us.

At the turn of the millennium we joined a team of 50 radical worshippers to fly around the world praying and worshipping in 12 strategic areas, Toronto, Canada; New Orleans; San Jose, CA; Wai Ka Ki Beach, Hawaii; Manila, PI; Hong Kong; Abu Dabi, UAE; Cairo, Egypt; many places in Israel, Rome, London, and Washington DC. In 2005 we flew to Brazil again to serve on another team healing the sick in *Vitoria, Espirito Santo.*

All of this was made possible by buying houses, fixing them up, and selling at a profit just as the Lord directed, before real estate prices rose. He made sure we bought at good prices and sold at the right time.

A Final Word from "Papa 'C'"

Ask yourself and God, "Where do we go from here?"

Give yourself to Him and dedicate yourself to fulfill His purpose for your life. This requires prayer, studying God's Word (The Bible) and becoming an active member of a church family that has a good vision for reaching the world.

Without a vision, the people perish," Proverbs 29:18, KJV

God is looking for those who will follow Him. The 12 apostles are a good example of this. Many people we talk to daily in our community are looking for a purpose and meaningful relationships in their lives. The plan God has for your life will be unique and perfectly suited for you. It will not be the same as ours.

We salute you as fellow travelers on the road of destiny! Keep in touch through our website: OurDestinyBook.com.

To Contact us, go to our website:
OurDestinyBook.com